Crisis in Law Enforcement

About the Author

Sankar Sen is presently Senior Fellow at the Institute of Social Sciences, New Delhi. He is a distinguished member of Indian Police Service from Odisha cadre. He served in the Intelligence Bureau for seven years and also as the Additional Director General of the Border Security Force. He was the Director of the SVP National Police Academy, (NPA) the premier Police Institution for training of IPS Officers in the country. As the Director of the NPA he was responsible for many innovative changes in the training programmes of Indian Police Service Officers. On completion of his assignment at the NPA, he joined as the first Director General of the National Human Rights Commission (NHRC) and later on functioned as the Special Rapporteur in charge of custodial programmes of the NHRC. He was instrumental in building up an excellent investigation wing of the NHRC. He was awarded the Police Medal for Distinguished Service in 1986. A large number of his articles on law enforcement, terrorism, human rights and trafficking etc. have appeared in national dailies and well-known magazines in and outside the country. His publications include *Indian Police Today, Police in Democratic Society, Human Rights in Developing Society, Terrorism and Drugs, Human Rights and Inhuman Wrongs, Trafficking in Women and Children, Enforcing Police Accountability through Civilian Oversight* etc.

Crisis in Law Enforcement

Sankar Sen, IPS

CONCEPT PUBLISHING COMPANY PVT. LTD.
NEW DELHI-110059

ISBN-13 : 978-81-8069-919-1

First Published 2012

Published and Printed by :

Concept
Since 1974

Concept Publishing Company Pvt. Ltd.
A/15-16, Commercial Block, Mohan Garden
New Delhi-110059 (India)
T: 25351460, 25351794, *F*: 091-11-25357109
E: publishing@conceptpub.com, W: www.conceptpub.com
Editorial Office: H-13, Bali Nagar, New Delhi-110 015, India.

Cataloging in Publication Data--*Courtesy:* D.K. Agencies (P) Ltd. <docinfo@dkagencies.com>

Sen, Sankar, 1936-
Crisis in law enforcement / Sankar Sen.
p. cm.
Includes bibliographical references and index.
ISBN 9788180699191

1. Law enforcement—India. 2. Law enforcement. 3. Police—India. 4. police. I. Title.

DDC 363.230954 23

Girish Chandra Saxena
Former Governor of Jammu & Kashmir

Foreword

Shri Sankar Sen, whose selected articles are being published in the form of this book, has come to be regarded by his peers as a top analyst and expert in matters relating to police, law enforcement and security and as an authority on the human rights issues. He is highly qualified to write on the subjects covered in the articles because of the varied and important assignments he was entrusted with by the government. Occasional articles appearing in newspapers generally have a passing or piecemeal impact, but a collection of informative and insightful articles on a wide range of a particular subject would generate a larger and more lasting picture. This book, therefore, will create greater awareness and better understanding of the problems and issues involved among the interested persons, the concerned professionals and administrative authorities and the political leaders.

Every article in the book is based on Shri Sankar Sen's personal experience or on his careful study of relevant facts. He is forthright in expressing his views and has the courage of his conviction to not mince words when he is sharply critical of something he considers to be wrong like torture, violation of human rights or inadequate response to the problem of corruption or crime against women, children and the elderly. He feels deeply for the victims of crime. He has unshakable faith in the primacy of means over ends. He invariably gives sound reasons for his opinions and suggestions.

One cause Shri Sen has espoused strongly in a number of his articles is the imperative and urgent need for implementing the essential police reforms, some of which have been included in the directions issued a few years back by the Supreme Court to the Central and State Governments for early implementation. Apart from its normal task of maintenance of law and order, prevention of crime and the investigation and prosecution of criminal cases, the police is presently facing several formidable challenges of great complexity like terrorism, religious fundamentalism, ethnic insurgency, left extremism and organized crime. These greater responsibilities have made the task of the police over the last three decades increasingly difficult and demanding. Further measures and reforms are required to be taken expeditiously for the police to become a truly modernized, well-trained, well-equipped, efficient and professional force from the police station level upwards, by giving the police autonomy in its functioning free from political interference, while ensuring its accountability through independent and broad-based mechanisms at the Central, State and District levels. Police stations which play a vitally important role in policing from the starting point must have adequate force levels, upgraded infrastructure and appropriate technological equipments. At the same time, the living and working conditions of the personnel of the para-military and state police forces require further improvement and the matter of police housing deserves greater and sustained attention. Meanwhile, all ranks of police can themselves do a lot more to better the image and credibility of the police force through their correct behaviour and attitude on all occasions, proper and prompt responsiveness, professionalism, imaginative and realistic approach to community policing and honest and courageous discharge of their duties without fear or favour.

I have every hope that this book will be well received and would serve its intended purpose.

Girish Chandra Saxena
Former Governor of Jammu & Kashmir

Contents

Introduction

The book contains a collection of articles covering various complex issues of law enforcement and the challenges faced by the police in dealing with them. Policing a democratic society is a difficult and complex job and police problems are compounded by constant political interference in police work. This has eroded police credibility and hampered their effectiveness in law enforcement and order maintenance. Recently, the Supreme Court has given directives for insulating the police from extraneous pressures, but there is reluctance of both Central and State Governments to implement the directives of the court. One of the articles in the book covers the subject. Not only the police but other segments of the criminal justice system are also in a poor state of health. Along with police reforms there is need for reforms of the criminal justice system. Police reforms also include better training, honest recruitment and inculcation of human rights culture in the force.

Articles dealing with Naxalite violence emphasise the moot point that battle against Naxalite terror has to be won by strengthening and galvanizing state police forces and not by placing overmuch reliance on the army. Better governance and improved law enforcement are effective antidotes to terrorist violence. Effective policing also depends upon closer understanding between police and the community. The article on community policing highlights the importance of this new strategy to fashion closer bonds between police and the community. Crisis in law enforcement faced by the country can be overcome by a carefully calibrated multi-pronged strategy and this is going to be a long haul. It is hoped that the articles will elicit the interest of law enforcement officers, academics and informed members of the public on diverse issue, concerning humane law enforcement.

Section I

1
Horror Killings

Horror killings of young couples by the relatives for intra-gotra or inter-caste marriages are being reported with sickening regularity from the National Capital Region and the adjoining states of Haryana, Punjab and U.P. A case of honour killing has also now been reported from Tamil Nadu. The National Commission of Women has correctly described them as "*horror killings*" as no honour is involved in these cruel acts of violence. The perpetrators of these crimes remain unrepentant and strongly feel that these crimes are justified to defend the honour of the family. The Supreme Court in the case of *Lata Singh* vs. *State of UP & Others* [2006 (5) SCC 475] FG urged stern action against the honour killers as provided by the law. The court said, "*There is nothing honourable in such killings and in fact they are nothing but shameful and barbaric acts of murder committed by brutal, feudal minded persons who deserve harsh punishments. Only in this way, we can stamp out such acts of barbarism.*"

Though many cases of honour killing are now being reported, a large number of cases also go unreported.

Further, the perpetrators are seldom punished. Honour killings are on the rise in India. In Muzaffarnagar, the worst affected district of Uttar Pradesh, 13 cases of honour killings were reported in the first nine months of 2003 against 10 in 2002. Further, 35 couples, were also declared missing during this period.

Honour killing is not however, a typical Indian phenomenon. It is being reported from various countries of the world. The United Population Fund (UPF) estimates that the annual worldwide honour killings victims may be as high as 5000. However, these figures may be the tips of the iceberg and not reveal the magnitude of the problem. In Pakistan, over the course of six years (1999-2004), four thousand women have fallen victims to this barbarous practice. Unfortunately, despite widespread condemnation, by human rights groups (HRGs), honour killings enjoy high level of support in Pakistani Society. Hima Jilani, a well-known human rights activist says "*Right to life of women is conditional on obeying social norms and traditions.*" An Amnesty International statement adds "*The regime of honour is unforgiving; women on whom suspicion has fallen are not given any opportunity to defend themselves and family members have no socially acceptable alternatives but to remove the stain on their honour by attacking the woman*".

So far there are no specific laws in the country to deal with honour killings. They are treated as murders. Many honour killings are socially sanctioned by caste panchayats and carried out by mobs with the connivance of family members. While mobs carry out the brutal attacks it becomes difficult to pinpoint the culprits and collect evidence. With the rising incidence of honour killing, there is urgent need for separate laws to deal with this crime. The Central Government intends to come out with new legislation. Under the proposed law, members of the *khap panchayat* or the victims' families if their actions result in a death of a person going against the wishes of the *khap* will be punishable with the sentence of death or life imprisonment. The crux of the changes proposed focus on placing the onus of proving innocence on the *khap panchayat* members and this includes not only the charge of murder but also the charge of abetting the offence. The amendment, if it made into law, will make all *khap panchayat* members associated with death accountable. The Home Ministry also intends to amend the Indian Evidence Act and Special Marriage Act and scrap the mandatory 30-days' notice period for a marriage, thus closing the window during which the couples are harassed and victimized by their relatives.

It is learnt that some Cabinet Ministers have found fault with the proposed law to deal with honour killings. They are of the view that charging and prosecuting all *khap* members for murders in case of honour killings will be difficult, if not impracticable. Some of them feel that existing laws provide strong deterrence, if the State Government has necessary will. Since law and order is a state subject, the Cabinet has decided to consult the State Governments and obtain their suggestions before bringing out a new law. The Prime Minister is not in favour of bulldozing a law through.

To deal with the menace, pro-active policing is also called for. In many cases of elopement, FIR alleging kidnapping are filed by the relatives of the girl and the police promptly oblige by arresting the boy. Though the police do not remain unaware of the dangers that await the couple when they return home, preventive action is seldom taken. The hard fact remains that caste and class bias which blind those perpetrating these crimes also at times infect the police. Failure to intervene effectively when such crimes likely to happen are within the knowledge of the police is inexcusable. Proactive policing and effective penal sanctions are best antidotes to this dishonourable practice. Delhi High Court judge Justice S.N. Dhingra rightly pulled up the police for its insensitivity and said that sometimes elopement cases are converted into rape cases. The police send the boy behind the bars on rape charges and allow the parents to kill the daughter.

In sum, honour killings are the outcome of a clash between tradition and modernity. Age-old norms in the society are being challenged by the younger generations who want to take their own decisions and not remain shackled by the norms of the past. Growing independence of women, is threatening the norms of the patriarchal society in which women are viewed as the property of the caste and the community and women's chastity is viewed as honour of the community. Women's honour is directly linked to their conformity to traditional and restrictive roles.

Mere passing of stern laws will not help unless public opinion through awareness campaigns is mobilized against this vicious practice. Our response to any serious social malaise is to pass a law and then forget about it. They remain unimplemented and clutter the statute books. Laws have to be enforced through state agencies and unless there is strong political will, enforcement of the laws will be tardy and half-hearted. In states like Haryana on pure electoral considerations, political parties do not want to lock horns with the *khaps*. No important leader has shown the gumption of denouncing the oppressive ways of the *khap panchayats*. This absence of political will further compounds the problem.

2

Guns and Goons: Arms Licence Only After Police Verification

The Arms Amendment Bill, 2010, intended to amend the Arms Act of 1959, has provoked unwarranted opposition. It was introduced in Parliament by the Home Minister. The National Association for Gun Rights, formed with Digvijay Singh, the former Chief Minister of Madhya Pradesh as the President, has criticised the Home Ministry for undermining the citizens' right to possess weapons. Singh is the patron-in-chief of the National Association for Gun Rights in India. In a memorandum to the Prime Minister, the association has alleged that under the pretext of moving a minor amendment to the Arms Act ostensibly to make police verification mandatory and create a database, the government is trying to undermine the citizen's legal right to keep and bear arms.

To own a gun is a privilege under the Arms Act, 1959. This particular legislation and the Arms Rules, 1962 were derived from the Arms Act, 1876, enacted by the British after the Revolt of 1857. It was intended to disarm a subject nation. To obtain licence for owning firearms, a person has to prove that "there exists a threat to life". A licence is limited to three firearms under Section 3 of the Arms Act, 1959.

Law-abiding citizens are entitled to possess arms, but the benefit of the 1959 Act has largely been reaped by dubious characters who have acquired sophisticated arms on a large scale. In view of the terror threat, the government has now decided to make the rules more stringent.

The new Bill's "Statement of Objects and Reasons" mentions that proliferation of arms and ammunitions, whether licensed or otherwise, can disrupt societal order and development, vitiate the law and order situation and lead to violence. This inherent danger needs to be curbed. It is imperative that arms licence is issued only to *bona fide* persons after their antecedents are verified by the police.

In reality, too many people possess arms licences. And for every licensed firearm, there are at least four or five unlicensed ones. According to a former Director-General of Police, U.P., there are more firearms, both licensed and unlicensed, with individuals in Moradabad district than in the whole of the UK or Japan. Both in Bihar and U.P., dacoits seize weapons from the licensed holders either by threatening them or on payment. The bulk of the ammunition used in country-made unlicensed weapons come from the license holders. The manufacture of ammunition is a complicated task, one that requires equipment, not easily available.

There is an increasing demand for guns in many areas of northern India, with Kanpur emerging as the "gun capital". Indeed, the gun is a status symbol. The Arms

(Amendment) Bill proposes to amend sub-section 13 of the Arms Act, 2009. It will specify the limit of 60 days from the date of receipt of application for sending the police report and to record the reasons for the failure to send the report within the deadline. The Bill omits the proviso to sub-section (2A) and Section 13 of the Arms Act, 1959 so as to do away with the discretion of the licensing authority to issue a licence without receiving the police report.

The problem of arms proliferation has assumed menacing proportions. The National Police Commission had recommended that arms and ammunition, be kept in safe custody to avoid their falling into the hands of unauthorized persons. Before issuing a licence, it should be ascertained that the applicant is in a position to keep them in safe custody.

Advocates of gun rights, such as Digvijay Singh and the young MP, Naveen Jindal, are trying to forestall the amendments that will tighten the Arms Act. They have perhaps been influenced by the prevailing gun culture in the USA. It is a contentious issue in America's politics and culture. At present, there are an estimated 240 million guns in America and about one-third of these are hand-guns which are easy to conceal. On an average, shootouts account for 30,000 deaths, including 12,000 murders, each year. "Since the killing of Kennedy in 1963, more Americans died in American gunfires than perished on foreign fields in the whole of the 20th century. (*The Economist*, April 21-27, 2007). The US Supreme Court, while ruling in the case of *McDonald* vs. *Chicago*, struck down a ban on the hand-gun. The ruling makes it unconstitutional for states and local governments to restrict the rights of the Americans to own guns. The court affirmed that Americans have the constitutional right, as enshrined in the Second Amendment, to own weapons including hand-guns. Gun control advocates, however, have slammed the ruling and described it as 'a victory only for the gun lobby and America's fading firearms industry'.

Japan and the UK are two democratic countries with very low crime and murder rates. Both countries have imposed a strict control on firearms. In Japan, possession of firearms is a rare privilege and the number of those who hold licences is limited. The bulk of the firearms are deposited in rifle and pistol clubs, and they cannot be moved out. This automatically restricts the firearms available with individuals. According to Chris Nuttal, former Director of Research, Home Office (U.K.), the argument of the gun lobby that it is the people – and not the guns – who kill people is not valid. The availability of guns escalates the risk of wounding or killing in every case of crime, including brawls in a pub or at home.

3
Gray Makes Vulnerable

Demographic ageing, a global phenomenon, has reached Indian shores too. It is time to focus on the issues arising out of people living longer and the rising grey population of the country. There are 70 million people above the age of 60 in India today, and this number is going to rise to 177 million by 2025. One of the many problems faced by elderly citizens, particularly in urban areas, is the fear of crime. This year has been particularly unfortunate for the elderly in Delhi. There were 11 cases of gruesome murder of older people, both male and female. The sensational double murder of Lieutenant General (Retd.) Harnam Singh Seth and his wife created widespread panic in the capital. However, a significant rise in crimes against the elderly has been noticed all-over the country.

Studies by criminologists in the West show that many older persons are reluctant to go to the police to report crimes against them for fear of reprisals. This makes them especially vulnerable to re-victimization. Research also indicates that the elderly endure far greater fear for their safety than is warranted by their actual victimization rates.

Various factors are responsible for the escalation of crime against the elderly. First, loneliness. Many old persons are forced to live alone and hence in the event of any attack or crime against them, do not get help immediately. Second is their dependence. Because of their inability to live on their own, they are forced to employ domestic help without first verifying their antecedents. This makes them vulnerable to attacks by criminals and other species of confidence tricksters. There are a number of cases, particularly in Delhi, of domestic servants involved in crimes against their employers.

Further, because of failing health, the elderly can be easily overpowered. Age magnifies the likelihood of victimization. Many of the elderly try to solve the problem by reducing exposure to potentially threatening situations. Because of crimes or the fear of crime, they do not venture out and develop a fortress mentality.

The elderly find the consequences of crime far more devastating than younger people, who have more years to overcome physical, mental and financial shocks. Broken limbs, as a result of encounters with criminals, or the loss of savings to a conman may diminish an older person's quality of life and make some of them live their last years in fear and distress. Elderly persons also remain susceptible to financial frauds. The FBI, in the United States of America, revealed a deliberate targeting of older persons by tricksters. Many of them have insurance, pensions, proceeds from the sale of a house, and other savings that make them attractive targets for criminals.

Many older people think that they are safe from crimes when they are in their house. But criminals use the telephone to trick people out of their savings. Telemarketing fraud is believed to cost Americans $40 billion a year and older people form a disproportionately large section of the targeted group. It is necessary to take senior citizens' fear of crime more seriously and find imaginative ways to improve their quality of life. It is aptly said that a society is judged by how well it protects its children and the elderly. The neglect of elderly persons' concerns, including their fear of crime, contributes to their belief that they are seen as being disposable and obsolete. The fear of crime, visible in the eyes of the elderly today, serves as a mirror of our future.

Elderly persons should necessarily follow a few security measures like going out in a group, keeping a dog as a pet, keeping vital telephone numbers handy, informing the police and neighbours if they are suspicious of someone, and insisting on getting their domestic servants verified by the local police. They should also try not to be a recluse, make an ostentatious display of cash and jewellery, trust strangers or open doors to unidentified persons, and ignore any suspicious incident.

Sometimes, law enforcement officers who contact the senior citizens are young and have little experience of working with the elderly. In the US, some police departments have created special positions called the law-enforcement gerontologists. They deal with the crime and abuse-related problems of the elderly and explore opportunities for the latter to contribute to crime-prevention programmes. By developing a rapport with the elderly, the officers identify their problems and then recommended ways to minimize the risk. They also alert the senior citizens about crimes being committed against the elderly.

In Japan, the elderly have been singled out for special outreach by the police. Police officers regularly telephone older citizens who live alone to check on their well-being. They observe "*silver days*" when policemen drop in at the homes of the elderly. Particular efforts are also being made by the Japanese police force to draw them into crime-prevention organizations.

Some of the initiatives by the police in India too deserve mention. The Mumbai police, with the help of non-governmental organizations like Dignity Foundation and Agni, have embarked upon programmes to prevent crimes against senior citizens. Under these programmes, officers visit the houses of senior citizens staying in the areas under their jurisdiction on a regular basis. There is also an Alert Citizen Watch scheme launched by Mumbai police, encouraging people to report crimes against senior citizens and the dangers of any crimes they might be exposed to.

Delhi police have also embarked upon innovative programmes to create a sense of security among senior citizens. Under this scheme, school-children are motivated to visit senior citizens on weekends to share their problems. The results so far have been encouraging. However, Delhi police's Servants Verification Scheme is going through a rough patch – attempts to get information from other states on servants working in middle-class localities in Delhi have drawn a blank. Residents are also reluctant to get their domestic help verified as they feel that the latter would feel insulted and leave. Perhaps community-policing, with an emphasis on face-to-face contact, may give the elderly their only access to help. For it is evident that the elderly need police protection to savour the golden years of their lives.

4
Spurt in Rape Cases in the Capital City

Rising incidence of rapes and gang rapes in Delhi has justifiably shocked and alarmed the citizens, particularly, women. An opinion poll survey shows that women, particularly in the age group, between 15-40, feel unsafe and fear-stricken in the streets of the capital. But recorded crime figures, paradoxically, show decline in cases of rape in Delhi. The data compiled by the National Crime Record Bureau (NCRB) show that in the entire country, 19,438 rape cases were registered in 2006 as against 20,737 in 2007 and 21,467 in 2008 (an increase of about 10.9 per cent between 2006 and 2008). Delhi witnessed a reverse trend; 658 cases registered in 2005, 623 in 2006 and 598 in 2007. Unfortunately, police statistics only reveal the tip of the iceberg. A large number of cases are either not reported or if reported not registered. However, the situation in this respect is not peculiar to India. The National Victims Survey in Australia found that only 32 per cent of victims of rape reported sexual assaults. In a study of undetected rape cases in Philadelphia in USA, conducted by S.C. Smithyman, it was found that of 100 rape cases, only 25 were reported to the police, 13 persons arrested and less than 5 convicted.

Admittedly, for a woman victim of rape, the experience is a shattering one and it takes for her years to feel normal again, if ever she does. "*You become afraid of*" writes, a victim, "*half the human race*". For an unmarried girl in our country such ignominy shatters her chances of ever getting married.

After the gang rape case in Mangolpuri, the Commissioner of Delhi police has decided to make police more visible and responsive by augmenting the strength of police pickets and increasing the number of PCR vans. However, just enhancing the strength and visibility of police will not stop crime or deter the criminals, particularly, the sex offenders. Instead of only increasing the police strength, the emphasis should be on quick police response to calls for help from harassed women. Very often, police response (*as reported in Mangolpuri case*) is slow and tardy. Again rapid response alone may not always help. In a path breaking research study, namely, Kansas City, Preventive Patrol Experiment, by the Police Foundation, Washington, it was established that randomized patrolling had a limited impact on crime and even in most cases, rapid response by the police did not help to solve the crime. In respect of a large number of offences the time taken by the public to report to the police was found to be the primary determinant of the eventual outcome.

Again empirical research studies have shown that majority of the rape cases are not sudden occurrences, but have been carefully planned and a large number of sex offenders are relatives, friends, and neighbours of the victims. However, rape by strangers, though few, are very violent in nature.

It is reported in the press that in the recent Mangolpuri gang rape case, the investigating officer has been replaced by a lady police officer, especially trained to handle cases against women. But by merely putting women officers in charge of investigation (as ordered by courts in many cases), will not help unless they are properly trained and adequately sensitized to sympathetically handle the traumatized victims. In my police career, I have come across women officers as insensitive as their male counterparts. Officers investigating into rape cases, on the contrary, must establish proper rapport with the rape victims and help them to overcome their sense of shame, nervousness and reluctance. Therefore, there is an urgent need for substantially augmenting the strength of women police officers in state police forces and particularly, in the investigating wings. Representation of women in police forces, in the country is less than 4 per cent and in Delhi it is 7.6 per cent of the total strength. But female officers in order to be effective have to be trained in supportive and sympathetic interviewing techniques. In sexual assault cases, the female victims feel embarrassed to answer probing questions by the male investigating officers and their failure to get detailed information from reluctant victims, in turn, weakens the cases.

There is shrill demand from many quarters to make anti-rape laws more stringent and provide death sentence to the rapists. But mere passing of stringent anti-rape laws will not reduce the crime. The Criminal Law Amendment Act, 1983, was passed as a response to the growing public opinion demanding stiff anti-rape laws. The Act amended Section 376 of the Indian Penal Code and enhanced the punishment of rape by providing that it shall not be less than seven years and if the sentence is less than seven years, the court will have to mention adequate and special reasons for this. It also provides minimum punishment of 10 years of imprisonment for police officers or the staff of judicial remand homes or other places of custody established by law. The Act also amended the Code of Criminal Procedures and provided for trial in camera. Unfortunately, passing of the stringent anti-rape laws did not reduce the volume of crime. Hence, it is wishful thinking that provision of death penalty for the rapists will serve as a deterrent. On the other hand, there is likelihood that because of enhanced punishment, the courts will analyze the evidence more closely and refrain from imposing the maximum penalty because of the fear of miscarriage of justice.

One of the tried and most effective ways of deterrence is quick trial and heavy punishment of the rapists. A study done by the Bureau of Police Research and Development reveals that the trial of rape cases prolongs for years thereby heightening the trauma of the victims. In many cases, the maximum punishment is not imposed by adducing some extenuating factors and lenient punishment is meted out to the perpetrators. In a well-known case, the court exonerated two young men of rigorous punishment because they had already suffered enough as under-trials. In a study of high rate of acquittals in rape cases in the Delhi courts, undertaken by the Institute of Social Sciences, the victims complained of lack of sensitivity displayed not only by the investigating officers but by the prosecutors. Another important factor behind failure of a large number of cases in courts of law is due to the negative opinion given by medical officers who examined the rape victims. Sexual assault cases are unique in that the police investigators have to rely on the examining physicians to collect the best evidence in the case, evidence from the body of the victims. In many cases, doctors in government hospitals refuse to give unbiased medical opinion in rape cases for fear of being cited as prosecution witnesses to be subjected to embarrassing cross-examinations in courts of law.

The Chief Minister of Delhi has suggested that women must learn to defend themselves when attacked by the rapists. But there can be no standard response to such attacks. In cases of aggressive resistance, there are instances of the rapist stabbing and fatally injuring the woman, who resisted. However, some knowledge of Judo and Karate could be useful in dealing with a lonely rapist, when attacked.

The Delhi Police must also go for victimization surveys to get a correct idea regarding the incidence of crime, particularly, crimes against women. Victimization surveys have become a regular feature of crime statistics in the United States. Such surveys also provide useful data as to why victims do not report crimes, yielding valuable insights into public attitudes and behaviour. Many criminologists justifiably regard victimization surveys as more reliable than crimes reported to the police.

5
Impermissibility of Narco Analysis, Polygraph and Brain Mapping Tests

The lawyers and human rights activists have welcomed the latest judgment of the Supreme Court that narco, polygraph or brain mapping tests cannot be conducted on anyone without their consent. In a significant ruling, the apex Court described the forcible administration of this test as an "*unwarranted intrusion*" on the personal liberty of a person accused of an offence. The court was deciding on a bunch of petitions filed by several accused persons including Godmother Shantokhben Jadeja and Arun Gawli against the use of narco analysis, brain mapping and lie detector tests on them as a part of the investigation. The court added that even in cases where a person voluntarily submits to undergo this test to establish his or her innocence, the National Human Rights Commission's "*Guidelines*" have to be observed.

The NHRC have published the guidelines for the administration of polygraph test (lie detector test) on an accused in 2000. These guidelines, *inter alia*, are:

- No lie detector test should be administered except on the basis of consent of the accused. An option should be given to the accused whether he wishes to avail such a test,
- The consent should be recorded before a Judicial Magistrate,
- During the hearing before the Magistrate, the person alleged to have agreed should be duly represented by a lawyer. The actual recording of the lie detector shall be done by an independent agency and conducted in the presence of a lawyer,
- A full medical and factual narration of the manner of information received must be taken on record.

The apex Court further observed that these tests are in contravention of the right to silence that an accused enjoyed. The Law Commission in its 108th report specifically warned the government against any dilution of right to silence in view of such trends in countries like UK. While dismissing the pleas of various state governments that the scientific methods should be supported in public interest for efficient investigation of criminal cases, the court said that "*questionable scientific reliability of these techniques comes into conflict with the standard of proof 'beyond reasonable doubt', which is an essential feature of criminal trials*". The Court further observed that "*If we permit forcible administration of these techniques, it could be the first step on a very slippery slope as far as the standards of police behaviour are concerned.*"

The judgment, as expected, has evoked critical response from police investigators and approbation from lawyers and human rights activists. Some senior police investigators are of the view that use of these techniques provide useful and critical leads in some cases. In Telgi Stamps scandal narco analysis, according to some CBI officers, did provide useful leads. Now as far as the CBI is concerned, the investigation in several cases where narco tests are pending would be hit. In Arusi case, the CBI took the permission of the Talwar couple before conducting test on them. It seeks the Court's consent only when suspects refuses to undergo narco analysis and investigators feel that it is crucial. Now refusal by the suspects would end the matter. After the Supreme Court verdict, the main accused in Ajmer Blast case Devendra Gupta has filed a petition in the local court seeking exemption from this test. Lawyers and civil rights groups, however have welcomed the judgment. Mumbai based senior lawyer Majid Memon has said that the judgment is important in the context of our country where many a time poor and innocent people are forced to speak against themselves. Lawyer Prashant Bhusan has dubbed narco analysis as a very "*imperfect and hazardous procedure which gives incorrect information.*"

Efficacy of narco analysis and other tests is often over-stressed by the police. The police are misguided to think the narco analysis is a boon to the police to make breakthroughs. The technique is neither modern nor internationally accepted one. Narco analysis, first captured attention when Robert House, a Texas obstetrician, used the drug scopolamine on two prisoners. These drugs are supposed to relax the individual defenses to the extent that he unwillingly reveals the truth he has been trying to conceal. Drugs like barbiturates, sodium pentothal have become the drugs of choice. But by 1950s, many scientists declared the notion of truth serum as invalid and many courts have ruled that testimony gained through them as inadmissible. It is true that barbiturates by disrupting defensive patterns can be somewhat helpful in interrogation, but even under the best of conditions they will elicit an output contaminated by deception, fantasy and garbled speech. According to a well-known forensic expert with considerable experience in participating in truth serum tests, these tests are occasionally effective on persons who, if they have been properly interrogated would have revealed the truth. On the other hand, the person who indulged in falsehood will be able to continue the deception even after the effects of the drug. Further wrong doses can send the subject into coma or even result in death.

Polygraph and Brain Mapping Tests

Apart from narco tests, there are two other kinds of tests, which are popularly used on suspects for extraction of truth, namely, polygraph and brain mapping tests. In polygraph test, the machine records the blood pressure, pulse rate and other bodily changes that are affected by a person's emotional conditions. Recorded changes are then studied, analyzed and co-related in response to specific questions and other stimuli. Results obtained from polygraph tests are not very credible as the device measures, body's reaction to different types of questions. The test is not scientific and "*inherently biased against the truthful.*"

Brain mapping test developed and patented in 1995 by neurologist Lawrence Farewell, is claimed to be an alternative to polygraph test. Here the subject is first interrogated to find out whether he/she is concealing any information. Then sensors are attached to the subject's head and the person is seated before a computer monitor. He is then shown certain images or made to hear certain sounds. The sensors monitor electrical activity in the brain and register p300 waves, which are generated only if the subject has connection with the stimulus, that is picture or sound. The subject is not asked any questions here. In America, the Federal Bureau of Investigation has been making use of "*brain mapping technique*" in criminal investigations.

This verdict of the Supreme Court now poses a challenge for police investigators and law enforcement officers. They will have to rely on diligent, painstaking investigation to unearth crimes and detect the criminals. The apex Court in this case has also pointed out that though the arguments of public safety "merit consideration", it is the task of the legislature to arrive at a "pragmatic balance between the competing interests of personal liberty of the accused and public safety."

6

Case of DGP Rathore – Lessons and Warnings

The despicable conduct of S.S.P. Rathore, former DGP Haryana has drawn universal condemnation. Media has brought to light the unsavoury details of Ruchika Girhotra's case and Rathore's high-handed and dubious means to delay the process of justice and harass the victim, leading to her suicide, and her family members. There is also vehement denunciation of the gross misuse of authority by the police. However, even in the midst of this country-wide uproar, it is necessary to separate the chaff from the grain and examine some of the issues thrown up by this tragic case carefully.

The charge of molestation against Rathore has been proved in the court of law and he has been convicted. There cannot be any doubt that the heinous offence was perpetrated by a senior police officer who is supposed to enforce law. It was witnessed by another girl, a friend of Ruchika, and the plea that both Ruchika and her friend have levelled false allegations against Rathore does not stand the glare of scrutiny. The criticism that the punishment meted out to Rathore is too little and too lenient is justified. But the hard fact to be borne in mind is that under the law (Section 354 of the IPC) the maximum punishment is 2 years' imprisonment with or without fine for the offence. The penal provision no doubt is inadequate. The punishment for child abuse should be far more deterrent. Indeed, Indian Penal Code of 1860 has often not kept pace with times. There is need to amend the Indian Penal Code and insert the offence of child abuse with proper definition and provision of exemplary punishment.

The case against S.S.P. Rathore has meandered along for nearly 19 years. This only highlights the malfunctioning of the country's criminal justice system in which the cases drag on interminably and the rich and powerful can cock a snook at it and delay the process of justice indefinitely. The facts of the case show that the police hierarchy, as is mistakenly presumed, did not try to protect Rathore. The then DGP, R.P. Singh, who conducted the enquiry in Sep., 1990, found substance in the allegation against the errant senior police officer and recommended registration of a criminal case against him. This was the correct thing to do because in departmental proceedings it is very difficult to sustain charges against a senior and powerful police officer who can always manouvre things in his favour. But the criminal prosecution could not be launched because of the powerful support Rathore got from the political boss, the then Chief Minister. It is this sordid nexus between police and the politicians, which provide immunity to the aberrant police officers and also help the political masters to terrorize and settle scores with their opponents. Hence, the need of the hour is to insulate the police from extraneous pressure and interference. Unfortunately, this point has not been properly emphasized in the media reports. For making the police accountable, it is necessary to emancipate it from constant political pressure and interference. Further, the politicians guilty of misuse of authority to shield bureaucrats should also be penalized. Otherwise, the cancer will fester and spread. A suitable amendment of the Representation of Peoples' Act for this purpose has to be thought of.

Ruchika's expulsion from the school for non-payment of fees was against all rules and norms. This happened because of unseen pressure on the school authorities. It is necessary to unearth why the school authorities took this harsh and punitive step and whether this was because of the malevolent influence of Rathore or due to pressures emanating from the Chief Minister's office. Normally school authorities do not so easily bow before pressure only from police unless backed by powerful extraneous elements.

Now, there is demand for prosecuting Rathore under Section 309 IPC for abetment to suicide. The CBI did not initially find adequate substance in the allegation, and opposed an application before the court for charging Rathore under this section. Now skeletons are tumbling out of the cupboards. According to a former Joint Director of CBI, as reported in the press, there was evidence to prosecute Rathore under Section 309 and Rathore tried his best to influence him and the CBI investigators. It is a crowning pity that he succeeded in this endeavour. The Punjab and Haryana High Court relied on CBI's stand before the trial court to conclude that no case of abetment of suicide was made out against the officer. In view of the materials now being unearthed, the case can be opened up for further investigation. Such investigation will serve an useful purpose as it will expose under whose pressure cases of car-theft were launched against Ruchika's brother and what was the role of investigators and supervisory officers. One investigating officer, according to press reports, has spoken of lack of evidence to arrest Ruchika's brother and charge-sheet him. The fact that he was hand-cuffed and paraded before the family members indicates that Rathore must have been pulling strings from behind to terrorize Ruchika's family.

Rathore has appealed against his conviction. In view of the public outrage, the appellate at Court will definitely look into the inadequacy of the punishment. It will also be worthwhile to examine the reasons for the progress of trial at snail's pace in the court of law and find out how many adjournments were given on what grounds and what other tactics were adopted to delay the process of justice. Speedy trial, as laid down by the Supreme Court, is a fundamental human right but many Judges unfortunately remain oblivious of it and do little to end the agony of the victims.

Rathore's case is just not an outrageous instance of abuse of power by senior police officer but also a glaring example of the havoc that can be wrought by police-politician nexus. The claim of the former Chief Minister Chautala that he removed Rathore from the post of DGP is not perhaps fully correct. This he had to do because the National Human Rights Commission objected to Rathore's continuance as DGP in view of the criminal prosecution pending against him.

Institutional mechanisms to insulate the police from extraneous influence, as prescribed by the Supreme Court in Prakash Singh's case have to be set-up without any delay. Of course, there will be stubborn opposition from the powers – that – be to curb their unfettered control over the police. There should also be strong condemnation from within the force of the likes of Rathore. There should be peer pressure to ostracize police officers who by their work and conduct sully the image of the force before the public. They may enjoy political patronage but lose forever respect and honour before members of the police. Peer influence is an important factor in ensuring rectitude in Japanese police. In Indian police service it is also necessary to inculcate similar restraining peer pressure and influence.

7
Erosion of CBI's Credibility

Move of the Central Bureau of Investigation (CBI) to close criminal proceedings against Ottavio Quattrocchi, has drawn flak from the Chief Metropolitan Magistrate, New Delhi. He criticised CBI's role in the investigation of the case against Quattrocchi and questioned its decision to approach Interpol for removal of the red corner notice against Quattrochi before obtaining court's permission for withdrawal of the case against him. Increasingly, CBI is losing credibility before the public as an independent investigating agency. This is a singularly unfortunate development that will seriously impede any meaningful efforts to combat corruption.

The CBI was set up under the Delhi Police Establishment Act (DPEA) in 1946. During its early years, the organization, under able and upright Directors, like D.P. Kohli, F. Arul enjoyed enviable reputation for transparency and professional competence. It selected its officers carefully and brooked no interference in its work. For IPS officers, deputation to the CBI was a prestigious assignment and they could function free from the pulls and pressures of the state politicians.

Decline of CBI and erosion of its credibility started during Emergency. The organization became politicized. The Shah Commission of enquiry which looked into the excesses perpetrated during the emergency severely indicted the role of the CBI in a number of cases. In some cases, it came to light that it was acting *mala fide* and had become an instrument of harassment of innocent people. The then Director of CBI, D. Sen was an officer of great professional competence and inspired fear and awe from the sub-ordinate staff. But he capitulated before the baleful pressures exerted by all powerful Sanjay Gandhi and his cronies and besmirched irretrievably the reputation of the organization. Shah Commission deplored the politicization of the organization and said that the fairness and objectivity with which an organization functions would in the ultimate analysis depend upon the extent to which the higher executives of the organization are allowed to function freely and objectively and at the same time ensuring their accountability to statutorily constituted bodies.

One of the main reasons for erosion of credibility of the CBI is political interference in its investigative functioning. Section 4 of the Delhi Police Establishment Act provides that CBI must function under the "superintendence" of the Central Government. Superintendence does not control or interference in the investigation conducted by CBI. In the case of *Vineet Narain* (1998) the apex Court held that Section 4 cannot be construed so as to prevent actual supervision of the investigation of an offence by the CBI and the Central Government is precluded from issuing any direction to the

CBI to curtail or inhibit its jurisdiction to investigate into offences.

Unfortunately, CBI has been functioning under successive Central Governments, as eminent jurist Fali Nariman has put it, "*not by notes on files but on nods or winks*" of the Minister or the senior bureaucrats in charge of the administrative Ministry. In cases of alleged corruption in the conduct of Commonwealth Games and handling up 2G spectrum by A. Raja, former Minister of Telecommunication, the CBI moved with disturbing slowness in taking necessary steps such as raids of houses of the officers and suspects, freezing their bank accounts, and their interrogation etc. The public cannot be blamed if it draws adverse inferences. Now it has been directed to investigate the 2G Spectrum case under the supervision of the apex Court. Unfortunately, in *Vineet Narain's* case (better known as *Hawala Case*) even under Court's scrutiny investigation was so inadequate, that charges could not be framed by the trial courts against the accused persons.

Indeed, much depends upon the mettle of the Director of the organization. He should be able to stand firmly against the nods and winks of the political masters. Now secure tenure of two years after selection as the Director, as enjoined by the court, gives him some elbow room. It is also the responsibility of the government to ensure, as the Shah Commission had recommended, that organizations like the CBI is led by competent self-respecting individuals, who are known for their appreciation of values and concern for the interests of the country and its citizens. "Lesser men as heads of such organization would only be a disaster".

Even now without extraneous interference, the CBI has done laudable investigation in cases relating to the assassination of Rajiv Gandhi in May 1991, and Mumbai's blasts of 1993 and in many other cases. Its performance has been acclaimed by all. To restore the credibility of CBI and make it an effective instrument for combating corruption there should be a comprehensive enquiry into the functioning of the CBI by an eminent professional of untarnished reputation or by a Joint Parliamentary Committee. The recommendations of such a committee have to be implemented in letter and spirit. At present, the annual reports of the working of the CBI's hardly figure in debates either in public or in Parliament. The CBI has to be insulated from extraneous pressures and made really independent. This has to be done by law expressly enacted by the Parliament. For this there are models in other countries which can be suitably adapted.

There are suggestions that the Director of CBI like CAG could be given an independent constitutional status. Another alternative is to keep CBI under the Parliamentary control. The Parliament would oversee the functioning of the CBI either directly or through a committee. The CBI on the pattern of the Australian model could be made accountable and answerable to this committee as adapted to Indian conditions.

Nearer home Independent Commission Against Corruption (ICAC) set-up in Hong Kong has done a remarkable job in reducing corruption and enabling Hong Kong to break out of its corruption trap. The government indicated its commitment by appointing a person of unimpeachable integrity as the Chairman and prosecuting some big fish. There is need for strong political will to make CBI independent, apolitical and effective.

Another factor sapping the efficiency of the CBI is that its charter has been widened to deal with various other forms of crime not connected with corruption. It is saddled with all kinds of cases that have nothing to do with corruption. The strength of the CBI in order to make it an effective instrument has to be substantially augmented. In 1996, the Federal Bureau of Investigation had 11,400 investigating officers while the CBI had only 1031. The Independent Commission Against Corruption (ICAC) whose activities are confined only to Hong Kong had as many as 684 investigators in its rolls. At present, CBI refuses to take over many cases but later on has to accept some of them either under court's orders or under the pressure of public opinion.

CBI's effective functioning suffers also because of constraints beyond its control. Monthly crime reports of CBI for the month of September, 2010, indicated that on 30.9.2010 as many as 9895 cases are pending for trial. Age-wise profile of the cases is the following:

Years < 2 years	*>2 years-5 <years*	*>5 years-10 <years*	*>10 years- <15 years*	*>15 years &<20 years*	*>20 years*	*Total cases pending under Trial*
2284	2475	2896	1190	645	405	9895

Source: Monthly Crimes Report of CBI of September 2010.

Again a number of cases are pending for prosecution sanction. As many as 108 cases are pending with Central

Government departments/authorities and 24 cases pending with state governments for sanction. Prosecution sanction was ostensibly meant for a check against non-appreciation of departmental procedures by an investigating agency or the court. So the department was given the discretion. But the influential and the forceful can manage its denial (as shown in the case of P.J. Thomas) and frustrate the ends of justice. This provision needs to be removed from the statute.

8

Flawed Recruitment, Training and Promotional Structure in the Police

At the Foundation Day ceremony of the Bureau of Police Research and Development (BPR&D), Delhi, the Union Home Secretary categorically stated that police recruitment in lower ranks is mired in corruption in most of the states. Police recruitment scam in many states, particularly in North India, is known to many. The Home Secretary is to be complimented for unveiling this scandalous state of affairs. In many states for recruitment in posts of constables, the candidates have to pay a bribe between rupees 1 to 4 lakhs. Many young boys are thus compelled to take heavy loans or mortgage their lands to pay bribes to the officials and politicians. Some time back, large scale irregularities and corruption in the recruitment of police constables came to light in Uttar Pradesh and exposed the sordid role of politicians and venal senior police officers in the recruitment of subordinate police officers and constables.

During the previous Samajwadi Party regime in UP altogether 22,000 policemen were recruited between the years 2004-06. Several irregularities in the recruitment including waving of police verifications to recruit the people with criminal records, forging examination papers and changing laid down procedures for selection of candidates came to notice. The same story has been replicated in many other states. Corruption in the recruitment of constables and lower subordinate staff is deplorable and reflects poorly on the functioning and leadership of the police in the states. Constables constitute nearly 80 per cent of police force at the cutting edge of law enforcement. The Committee on Police Training 1973 (better known as Gore Committee), observed that "recruitment procedures should be so devised that they are free from political, personal and other corruptive influences. The need for objectivity in selection cannot be over- emphasized."

In UP, it is reported that a private firm was hired to check the objective types of answer sheets. In several answer sheets whitener was used to erase old answers. Similar *modus operandi* was detected in the selection of candidates of a paramilitary organization of the Central Government. Fortunately, this time Mayawati Government in UP did learn the lesson and recruitment of nearly 30,000 police officers and men was done in a fair and transparent manner and no malpractice or corruptive methods could be detected. In this connection, it can be mentioned that some states like Karnataka, Andhra Pradesh and Rajasthan have already streamlined recruitment procedures which by and large are immunized from outside pressures. Thus, given the political will, there is no reason as to why this will not be possible in other states. Otherwise, prevalent system of malpractice and corruption in police recruitment will sound a death knell for police integrity and discipline.

Unfortunately, not only recruitment but police training also remains in a very bad shape. Training has remained, as described in the report of the Gore Committee, "*a ritual where unwilling and ill-equipped instructors are performing the rites of training and drilling to the unwilling trainees*". Most of the state training institutions are becoming dumping grounds for inefficient and corrupt officers who transmit wrong and negative values to the trainees. The trainers must enjoy an honoured position in the institutions so that they can play the role of change agents. The Gore Committee recommended suitable incentives including rent-free accommodation, special pay, recognition in the form of subsequent promotions and good postings for the trainers with a view to attracting the best available talents. Unfortunately, except in some central training institutions these incentives have not been made available to the trainers. Very often postings in training institutions are viewed as a punishment.

As the Director of National Police Academy, I visited different police training institutions in UK and USA. I found that, unlike in India, the job of trainers in police training institutions was a prestigious one and there was a long list of officers willing to serve. Trainers not only had excellent teaching and communication skills, but also wide-ranging police experience. They, thus brought into the training process the necessary wisdom and experience to bridge the gap between theory and practice.

For effecting any real improvement in police work on the ground that there should be utmost stress on proper and intensive training of police personnel. However, training, though essential, is not the only input for improving and optimizing work performance and effecting attitudinal transformation of officers and men. Training can be effective, provided the organization has faith in it and the organizational climate encourages the observance of precepts taught during training. A heavy responsibility thus rests on the senior officers to build a congenial organizational climate.

Further, for any worthwhile improvement in the working of the police, it is absolutely necessary to bring about qualitative changes in the duties of the police constables who constitute almost 70 per cent of the police force. The constables of the present day have moved far from the predominantly mechanical role assigned to them by 1902 Police Commission. They have to interact with the public in a variety of situations where they have to apply their mind and exercise judgment and enforce law with public understanding and cooperation. Today, they cannot function as automations in situations, requiring exercise of discretion and judgment. Any restructuring of the police system will not be enduring unless the mass base of the pyramid is rendered healthy and efficient.

A large number of the constables retire in the same rank after 32 or 35 years of service. They do not get even one rank promotion in their service careers. Promotional structure in the police system is thus not conducive to the fulfilment of legitimate career and ambitions of the constabulary.

The police constable must cease, as a perceptive scholar has suggested, to be a spear-carrier in the background of the police drama. He must be a major actor standing in the centre stage. It is essential that Indian police in order to be effective should have greater number of highly trained constables capable of assuming responsibilities in day to day affairs. This development was the essence of Sir Robert Peel's Reform of the London Police Force in the 19th century.

The Second Administrative Reforms Commission in its report on "*Public Order*" has strongly advocated the need to upgrade skills and training of the constabulary. It recommended that instead of recruiting constables who are matriculates, it will be better to recruit graduates at the starting point of civil police and give them the nomenclature of Assistant Sub-Inspector. It calculated that 700 graduate Assistant Sub-Inspectors can be recruited annually against a vacancy of about 1000 constables without extra financial burden. This would improve police performance at the base and help more effective police coverage of the country. Complete stoppage of recruitment of Constables may entail some practical problems, but reduction of their number and replacement by more qualified Assistant Sub-Inspectors of police is a sound practical proposition.

9

Order and the Law

Law enforcement and order maintenance is the prime responsibility of the police in any society. The word "Police" is derived from Latin word politia, which stands for state or administration. Police is the main agency through which preservation of peace and order is ensured by the government. The job of the police is difficult, hazardous and can be unbelievably thankless. Indeed, from no other profession, so much is demanded which so little recompense. Police profession also lionizes toughness and machismo qualities, necessary for ceaseless battle against the forces of lawlessness and disorder. This stern message was continuously drummed into our ears during our training as probationers days at the Central Police Training College, Mt. Abu. We were told that the police service was not for the weak and faint-hearted and not for the people with namby pamby thoughts and utopian ideas. The war against crime is unending, a Sisyphean task meant only for the tough and undaunted.

During my period of practical training as Assistant Superintendent of Police, Cuttack, some of the old war horses, including my SP, repeated the same adage and asked me to forget what had been taught in the training school and adjust myself to the stark ground-realities. The dominant police view is that, "*ends justify the means*" and for ensuring that criminals get their just deserts, the police, if necessary, should bend rules and get round laws and not hesitate to practice what is called "*noble cause corruption*". Good policing is not possible by acting within the four corners of law.

Fortunately, during that period, I have had the opportunity of coming in close contact with the then Chief Justice of Orissa High Court, R.L. Narasingham. He was a member of the Indian Civil Service (ICS) but opted for the judicial side. Short and gaunt with sparkling eyes and smiling face, he was a simple man unaffected by the dazzle and majesty of the service he belonged to.

The first day I met him at the Cuttack club, his immediate question was why I do not come for playing tennis-*a de-rigeur* for an Assistant Superintendent of Police. I mumbled some excuses, but there was no escape. Narasingham used to come regularly to play tennis in the club. I used to get calls from his Registrar that His Lordship wants me to come to the club to play tennis that too in proper kit. Thus, began my initiation in tennis. The tennis marker of the club Pankaj gave me many useful tips and I was able to pick up the game tolerably well within a short time. This proved to be a boon in my long service career. Later on, as the Director of the National Police Academy, I played and enjoyed tennis with the IPS probationers and thereby forged a close understanding with many of them.

However, to go back to my Cuttack days, I also had the chance of long and interesting *tête-à-tête* with Justice Narasingham after the games. He had a sharp analytical mind and his observations on contemporary events and *dramatis personae* in Orissa's political firmament were both incisive and insightful. He also recounted with evident glee, interesting anecdotes, including, scandals about some of the leading lights of the club. Because of his civil service background, he was quick in taking decisions, a quality missing in many in judicial fraternity. I shall always remember one of his many memorable aphorisms which later on I have repeated to many of my junior colleagues and probationers. He asked me to always remember as a young police officer that the role of the police is to maintain law and order, but order through law, otherwise, dacoits any day could maintain better order than the police.

Over the years, I came to understand and appreciate the importance and import of this insightful observation and tried to adhere to it to the best of my capacity. It helped me immensely in my discharge of duties. In police job, one has to constantly encounter the dregs of society, the scum of earth and witness man's inhumanity to man. Many policemen, says Berkley criminologist, Gordon Misner, "*Picture themselves as crime fighters standing against the Mongol hordes without the support of the public, politicians or courts*". This misconceived zeal makes them think that the hardened criminals will not respond to normal methods of investigation and detection and so they resort to practices, which are downright questionable and illegal. But this, without doubt, is a perverted and wrong approach. Crime is contagious, and there will be utter contempt for law if police themselves become the lawbreakers. In any democratic society, law vests vast powers in the hands of the police to curb lawlessness of anti-social elements, but also keeps provisions to ensure that these powers are not misused or abused to imperil the freedom of the citizens. The mandate of the police to use force to curb violence raises the key issue that police themselves should not indulge in unnecessary or excessive use of force. Lawless police is an abomination in a free society. It is mistakenly argued that to control dreaded criminals or terrorists, tough policing involving violation of laws and rules is necessary, if not unavoidable.

With my long years of experience in active policing, I have always felt that this is an erroneous argument, and there is always the danger of police officers sliding down the slippery slope. Once a certain degree of force is permitted, the police officers face an overwhelming temptation to apply as much force they consider necessary to obtain the sought-after information. I have seen promising careers of young police officers coming to a sad end on account of transgressing laws and perpetrating illegalities due to the mistaken notion that end justifies the means. In any conflict of ends and means, the point to be borne in mind is that if the ends are important enough to justify the means. Conviction of a criminal is important, but more important is the fact that in a liberal democracy, the police are expected to carry out their activities in a manner that advances the value of a liberal society. Adoption of impermissible means may ultimately undermine the end. The Independent Commission of Police in Northern Ireland (Patten Commission) has aptly said that "*bad application or promiscuous use of power to limit a person's human rights by such means as arrest, strip-and-search, house searches, can lead to bad police relations with the entire neighbourhood, thereby rendering in effect policing of those neighbourhoods impossible*". Adoption of unlawful means damages the standing of the police and also their effectiveness. To my mind, Narasingham's perceptive words sum up the essence of law enforcement and order maintenance – core functions of the police.

Section II

10

"Broken System": Report of the Human Rights Watch

The report of the Human Rights Watch on Indian police titled "*Broken System – dysfunction, abuse and impunity in the Indian police (August 2009)*" is a slashing indictment of the prevailing police system in the country. It pitilessly exposes some of the grave ills afflicting the police organization all-over the country. The report details many instances of police highhandedness and brutality, specially targeted against the poor and downtrodden sections of the society. Many of the infirmities and abuses highlighted in the report are well-known and have been documented in many other reports and discussed "*ad nauseam*" in seminars and meetings, but little concrete action has been taken by the government as well as the police leadership to set things right. In consequence, Indian police remains frozen in time, an alienated force serving the politicians in power and not the people of the country.

The Human Rights Watch report rightly spotlights on the poor and depressing conditions in which the police officers and men work in the field and the woeful lack of amenities in the police stations and outposts. It says that many police stations in rural areas lack electricity and in hot summer the police officers work outside in the courtyards to get some respite. There are no generators or power back-ups. Long hours of work (15-16 hours a day) without any overtime allowance, absence of recreational facilities and abysmally poor housing conditions demotivate them, sap their working capacity and efficiency and exercise a coarsening effect.

There is acute shortage of police personnel in India. There are approximately 122 policemen per 1 lakh of population, which is far below the police population ratio in peaceful and advanced countries of the West. In states seriously affected by the Naxalite violence like West Bengal, Orissa, Jharkhand, it is even less then 100. India has four times as many people for each policeman as the United States and Great Britain. What is more, the ratio improves markedly for urban areas. The rural countryside with its vast expanses remains neglected.

The National Police Commission in its report (first report 1978) elaborately dealt with the problem of police housing. As against the general principle enunciated 150 years ago (Report of the Police Commission 1860-62) regarding provision of 100 per cent accommodation for the Non-Gazetted Police Personnel, the actual position in the field is that more than 50 per cent of non-Gazetted Policemen all-over the country had not been provided with government accommodation of any kind whatsoever. Many of them particularly in urban areas, live in slums side by side with anti-social elements. Of late, both Central and

State Governments have taken some feeble steps to improve the housing facilities of the police but they just remain drops of relief in an ocean of distress. During my tenure in the National Human Rights Commission, I was appalled to find that there are police stations in some north Indian states without lockups and prisoners are tied by ropes with trees so that they cannot escape.

The report details many shocking atrocities committed by police in states like UP, Karnataka etc., and the lack of human rights culture that permeates the entire police organization. It seems that disquieting statements of the victims recorded in the report, even allowing for some embellishments, are by and large true. The National Human Rights Commission receives on an average more than 70,000 complaints annually and 50 per cent of them are against the police. Unfortunately, the victims of police highhandedness are mostly from the poor and marginalized groups living on the fringes of the society.

The report is not correct in saying that there is a culture of impunity and a total lack of accountability. During the year 2007 disciplinary inquiries were initiated against 19,187 police personnel and 665 policemen were either dismissed or removed from service. Major punishments were awarded to 4,650 and minor punishment to 15,275 police personnel. (Report of the National Criminal Records Bureau, 2007). However, it is also a fact that a large number of complaints against the police are not registered. Along with massive burking of crime, there is also massive burking of complaints. In some bad cases venal police officers have been convicted and punished by courts but such cases are not many. This is because it is difficult to substantiate allegations against the police. Besides the "*blue code of silence*" among the police officers themselves, witnesses feel scared to depose against the police. As a result, charges in many cases levelled against the police remain unsubstantiated. Similar difficulties have also been experienced by police complaint bodies in countries like UK, Canada, Australia etc. Complainants feel disenchanted when they find that civil oversight bodies also exonerate policemen for lack of evidence.

The Human Rights Watch report rightly emphasizes the lack of political will to reform the Indian police. Comprehensive reforms of the Indian police have been in the national agenda for more than 30 years. The National Police Commission established during the Janata Party's post-emergency government recommended comprehensive structural reforms of the police, but the government did not implement them. The report of the NPC was kept in the back burner. At long last, the Supreme Court in Prakash Singh's case had issued clear seven-point directives to the Central and State Governments to introduce some of the major reforms recommended by the NPC for insulating the police from extraneous pressures and making it more accountable and citizen-friendly. The report of the Human Rights Watch has also mentioned how the Central and State Governments are dragging their feet and trying to scuttle the court's directives by various devious strategems.

Soli Sorabji Committee appointed by the government drafted a new Police Act in 2005 to replace the old Act of 1861. The new Act seeks to set-up a modern police force reliant on community's support. However, the bill remains on the anvil of the Parliament and the government is in no hurry to pass a new Act. Some of the State Governments (like Bihar) have passed Acts, which are palpably retrogressive and seek to strengthen indirectly further political control over the police.

Again many states have not complied with the apex Court's directives, but the court has not initiated contempt of proceedings against the non-compliant states. The court had set-up a monitoring committee to review state's compliance but unfortunately the committee has not set-up any timetable and is working at a snail's pace.

The report deplores lack of training of the police in investigative skill and techniques. This is not an exactly correct picture of the situation. Professional training for crime investigation is given to senior and junior police officers in central and state police training institutions. There are capable investigating officers in many state police forces but the pressure to produce quick results from the public and political bosses and the malfunctioning of the criminal justice system as well as the legal handicaps under which the police continue to function are some of the contributory factors behind abusive and coercive investigation. The report skirts round these issues. Police reform will not be possible without reforms in the existing criminal justice system. Some of the important recommendations of the Malimath Committee for reforms in the criminal justice system cry for quick implementation.

One of the grossest violation of the human rights by the police, as mentioned in the report, is non-registration of the cases. On a very conservative estimate at least 50 per cent of the cases are not registered by the police. Human Rights Watch recommends change in police manual rule to make failure to register FIR, ground for disciplinary action. This is so even now and the defaulters can be booked under Section 29 of the Police Act. But it fails to note that the rub lies elsewhere. At present, on the basis of concocted police statistics the performance of the State Governments in maintaining in law and order is judged on the floor of the State Assemblies and Parliament. Any Chief Minister will frown upon free registration of cases showing sharp escalation of crime as that will show in a poor light law and order situation in the State. No DG of police will dare to incur the displeasure of the Chief Minister and risk his job.

The National Human Rights Commission recommended establishment of District Complaint Authorities to ensure speedy enquiry into complaints against the police and speedy relief to the victims. Similar directives had been issued by the Supreme Court in the case of Prakash Singh. But both the State Governments and police leadership are unwilling to establish such mechanisms on the specious plea that this will go to demoralize the police. They forget that an accountable police will command greater respect and co-operation from the public than an unfriendly and unaccountable police. Totalitarian states are called police states because the police remain beholden to certain individuals and groups and remain vulnerable to pressures from them.

The tragedy of Indian police is that it has remained the ruling party's police and not the people's police. It remains beholden to the political masters and alienated from the public. Without meaningful reforms to insulate the police from political pressures and influence Indian police will remain dysfunctional, a prisoner of the past. The present attempts just to tinker with reforms will not help.

The report does not take notice of the fact that there are a large number of upright, conscientious police officers in all ranks who are rendering yeoman service against titanic odds. A large number of policemen are sacrificing their lives in line of duty. Apathy of the civil society to the problems and constraints of the police and the systemic malaise that is eating into its vitals is painful. Good governance of the country will remain an utopia without meaningful police reforms.

11

Dantewara Massacre: Lessons and Warnings

Brutal killing of 76 CRP personnel including a Deputy and Assistant Commandant by the Maoists is a game-changer. It reveals the organizational strength, the level of preparedness and the savagery of the Maoists and sends a grim message that the paramilitary forces and the state police are not fully trained and equipped to take on them.

CRPF personnel were ambushed in the thick of Mukrana forest in Dantewara District of Chhattisgarh. A major portion of Dantewara district of South Bastar is a so called a liberated zone where there is hardly any physical presence of the civil government. The Maoists run a parallel government of their own. It seems that CRPF men fell into a well-laid trap. Reports indicate that some wrong information about the Maoists' training camp inside the deep forest area was planted and the CRPF men of 62-battalion went to the forest for a raid. They came under withering fire while returning to the base camp. Anticipating that once under fire CRPF men would seek cover under rocks and trees, the Maoist had planted pressure mines under these features. As anticipated, many

CRPF men seeking cover under rocks and trees when firing began were blown up by mines and others were shot by the Maoists who had surrounded them. Events raise fears that there could be moles in the CRPF camp.

In anti-Maoist operations, the CRPF have to work jointly with the local police who are familiar with the terrain and the forest routes. Unfortunately, only two senior constables were accompanying them. This clearly indicates that there is lack of proper coordination between the CRPF and the local police. It was hardly a joint operation as claimed by the Home Minister. Now a former DG of BSF and a very capable officer, Shri Rammohan has been asked by the government to enquire into this ignominious episode. It is hoped that the report will reveal the sequence of events and the operational blunders.

The cold-blooded massacre of the CRPF jawans has provoked widespread indignation against the savagery of the Maoists. There is insistent demand from many quarters for using the army and the air force for anti-Maoist operations. But any knee-jerk reactions instead of helping will further compound the problem. The time for rhetoric is over and a very clear and hardheaded strategy for countering the Maoist threats has to be worked out

Maoists today are a far cry from the ill-equipped Naxalites of the 1970s. They are highly organized and motivated. Their leaders are young and they have nearly 22,000 armed cadres spread over seven states. They had an annual budget of 60 crores in 2007, 42 crores were earmarked for purchase of arms and ammunition and explosives and Rs. 2 crores for intelligence. Their collection has now significantly increased. Extortions from contractors, mine owners, *tendu* leave traders, and sandalwood smugglers are their main sources of funding. Though the notion of red corridor from Andhra to Nepal is exaggerated, it has to be admitted that the Maoists had been able to significantly expand their areas of militancy during the last few years. Unlike terrorism in Jammu & Kashmir and the North-east, which are border-states, Maoism is threatening to spread into the country's heartland which is considered as its treasure trove. They have got nearly 100 training camps and many of their armed cadres are reportedly being trained by ex-army officers.

Paramilitary forces particularly the CRPF, is in the forefront in the operations against the Maoists. CRPF though a trained and disciplined force, has virtually no experience in jungle warfare. For them, as admitted by its senior officers, it is an unfamiliar operation in an unknown terrain. They have to be trained and inoculated in jungle warfare to give battle to an enemy living in forests over years and who have thorough knowledge of the terrain. Hence, in the area domination operations some operational omissions leading to irreparable loss of lives are inescapable. However, lessons have to be learnt quickly and mistakes should not be repeated.

Chidambaram has said that though the government had not so far used air power against the Maoist insurgents but if necessary, it will revisit the mandate and make necessary changes. Use of air power may not be on the cards given the risk of collateral damage and objections of the air force. But air crafts can be used for surveillance, reconnaissance and pinpointed operations. The government agencies have just started using Unmanned Aerial Vehicles (UAVs) to survey the affected areas, locate hideouts and send messages to the nearby forces to mount counter attacks. But these flying machines will not be of help unless they have powerful infrared equipped cameras to photograph the targets through thick foliages and mist covers.

Dantewara massacre has now emboldened the Maoists. They feel that they can take on the state forces and defeat them. They have warned of more attacks and in a letter, which they have now circulated they have urged the family members of the security personnel participating in anti-Maoists operations to call them back home. They are brazenly trying to subvert the loyalty of the paramilitary forces.

For the security forces and their political masters this is the time to steady the nerves and not press the panic button. State police and paramilitary forces of the Central Government acting in tandem can successfully thwart the Maoists without involving the army. It was the police and the paramilitary forces which thwarted the terrorists in Punjab. In Andhra Pradesh, the police and its specialized units like the Greyhound have been able to effectively tackle the Maoists. In Andhra, Maoist incidents fell from 576 in 2006 to 62 in 2009. Killings by the Maoists from 211 to 17 and police deaths from 25 to zero. The key to success is purposive police action backed by intelligence. Tripura police has also done a commendable job in tackling the insurgents. Lessons for other states affected by the Maoists are clear, Police forces have to be trained, modernized and functioning of the intelligence apparatus improved so that they can penetrate the Maoist groups. Time has also come to work out swift intelligence-based operations targeting the Maoists in their hideouts. This will dent their capability and morale and put them in disarray. This will also erode their support among the local population.

There is also need for proper coordination between the centre and the states to carry out well, directed and well-planned strategy against the Maoists. Operation *Greenhunt* has not been so far very successful because some of the states are dragging their feet due to political and electoral considerations. However, reports from the field indicate, despite some constraints the operation *Greenhunt* in West Bengal and Jharkhand border has been able to create confidence in the minds of the locals in Purulia (West Bengal) and Ghatsheela (Jharkhand) areas. Local villagers are coming forward to inform on the Maoists.

Training of the police and paramilitary forces has to be significantly improved and upgraded. Police training institutions in most of the affected states are in a poor shape. Further, each state has armed police battalions, but they are ill-trained and ill-equipped. Eastern Frontiers Rifles was once an elite force but now, as attacks on Silda camp has shown, it is ill-trained and poorly led. The same is true of most of the armed police battalions in others states affected by Maoist menace. CRPF has also to train its men in jungle warfare thoroughly. Hurried training course for 20 or 30 days in army training schools is not adequate. There should be a certain percentage of men earmarked for training. At present, this is not happening because constant deployment of CRPF on various duties. If this trend persists, CRP will also go the way of other state armed police battalions.

12

Army Deployment in Combating the Maoists

The decision of the Cabinet Committee of Security not to use the army in a combat role in the operations against the Maoists is welcome. The Home Ministry has been pressing for some time for a more active role of the army. The earlier proposal to deploy Rashtriya Rifle Battalions of the Army in some of the affected areas was not accepted by the army on grounds of insufficiency of troops. It was also felt that this will expand the areas of conflict, cause avoidable collateral damage and spawn other problems. When the proposal was initially mooted by the Home Ministry, the AIR Chief Marshall Nayak had pointed out that Army, Navy and Air Force are not trained for limited lethality.

Already army is overstretched and its reluctance to be dragged into another internal security duty beyond the existing ones in J&K and North-east is justified. While answering a question in Parliament, a few years ago, the Defence Minister had averred that 1,20,000 army personnel are deployed for counter-insurgency operations. In addition, 65 battalions of the army's counter-insurgency force – Rashtriya Rifles had been deployed in J&K and 31 out of

46 battalions of the Assam Rifles in the North-east. The secondary role of internal security duty does hamper the army's primary role of defending the country against external aggression. Prolonged deployment for internal security duty reduces rest and recoup tenures of the army and affect their efficiency and morale. The anti-Maoist operations are going to be a long-drawn affair and will need prolonged deployment of the army over vast forest areas. There are also other complexities. The army has pointed out that the troops cannot be deployed for active operations without adequate legal protection through the implementation of The Armed Forces Special Powers Act (AFSP) and other related instruments. Again, the Maoists will not be unhappy if the armed forces are deployed against them. It will be an acknowledgement of their power and reach and will add to their aura of invincibility. They will fabricate stories of army's atrocities as the insurgents have done elsewhere to further demoralize the troops. Tribal populations in many affected areas will be alienated.

The Home Ministry also wanted de-mining operations as one of the important tasks to be assigned to the army, but the army's view is that the de-mining cannot be segregated as an operational task since no area is permanently mined. The Maoists make use of mines and IEDs as and when they feel necessary and hence the forces operating in the areas have to develop own capacities for de-mining operations.

So far the Centre's operational strategy has been to concentrate its forces in the areas of Maoist domination and attempt to reclaim the areas from them. But the

Maoists constitute a faceless enemy who will never confront the state in its areas of strength. In campaign of attrition, they target the areas where the force is dispersed or the strength of the force is reduced.

A revised strategy is now being worked out by the government to confront the Maoists. The involvement of the army will by and large be limited to the training of the personnel of the police and para-military forces, particularly in jungle warfare.

Meanwhile, the Maoist threat has become more serious and sinister. The current attrition rate in the counter-insurgency operations favours the Maoists. It is estimated that 170 security forces personnel were killed as against 108 Maoists during the first five months of 2010 and in 2009, 312 security forces personnel were killed as against 204 Maoists. It is also seen that the earlier reluctance of the Maoists not to target innocent civilians is yielding place to senseless violence and callous disregard for civilian lives with a view to discrediting the governments, and creating a feeling in the minds of the people that the state authorities are not in a position to protect them.

In any effective counter insurgency operations against the Maoists, the police has to be given primacy. Experience of counter-terrorist operations in different parts of the country shows that the police have to be in the forefront of successful operations against the terrorists. In states like Punjab, Andhra, and Tripura where anti-Maoist operations have been successfully conducted, the police have played a leading role. The final responsibility for the maintenance of peace and order and countering the terrorists was vested in the Superintendent of the Police in the district. The army and paramilitary forces, wherever deployed co-operated and co-ordinated with the strategies evolved under the command of the police. Of course, there was vast augmentation of police strength and capabilities through training, acquisition of weapons and equipments, mobility and fortification of the police stations. Trained, well-drilled and well-equipped Anti-Terrorists Units (Greyhound in Andhra) were set-up to conduct intelligence-based operations against the enemy. These successful operations threw the Maoists off-balance and put them in disarray. Small mobile units were better able to move in jungles and launch surprise attacks. The police were able to gather better and more reliable intelligence from the local people than the personnel of the army and paramilitary forces who do not belong to the area. In this connection, the fact to be borne in mind is that the counter-terrorism and counter-insurgency operations are small commanders' war and they have to be empowered. Force capabilities at Thana, Post, Company and Platoon level (in the case of CPMFs) have to be strengthened. They must have adequate tactical and technological capabilities to respond promptly and adequately.

Unfortunately, police forces in many of the states rocked by Maoist terrorism are in a poor state of health. There are a large number of vacancies at police stations and supervisory levels. Police forces have to be quickly revamped, retrained and de-politicized and this is not going to be an easy job. There is unwillingness of State Governments to carry out police reforms and implement the directives of the Supreme Court in the case of *Prakash Singh* vs. *Union of India*. Most of the States have not so far segregated law and order and investigative functions of the police.

To tackle the Maoists, the State could either follow "*drying-up the swamp*" approach by gaining control of the areas like Bastar, Malkangiri etc. or adopt "*outsider-in*" approach by stabilizing the moderately affected areas and then trying to converge on the most troubled areas. Perhaps the latter approach will bring greater dividends because it would be possible to deploy government resources properly and judiciously to improve the lot of the common people and win them over. In Andhra, roads, police stations, schools and government offices were created in the northern forest belt adjoining Chhattisgarh. The State had reclaimed these areas earlier occupied by the Maoists. Thus, for successfully combating the Maoist menace in the affected states there is need to modernize police force and revamp intelligence apparatus. There is need for building of roads and improve the range and quality of government services. This will require not only massive central funding but also close coordination between the centre and affected states. Unfortunately, the required coordination and identity of approach is missing.

In Tripura also the police and the security forces have been able to contain three decades old insurgency in the state. The Chief Minister of State, Manik Sarkar provided excellent political leadership. Armed action was followed by appropriate socio-economic measures to alleviate the distress of the common people. There was constant endeavour not to allow human rights violations by the security forces.

The success of the Maoist operations is causing concern outside the country. Fears and misgivings were expressed by security experts in the Asian Security Conference at Singapore regarding the security of India's nuclear arsenal if the country is unable to reverse the success of the Maoists. It was pointed out by the National Security Advisor, Shiv Shankar Menon that the Maoist threat though serious, should not be exaggerated. It is a rural-based insurgency with little support in the urban areas and it is an Indian movement with an Indian agenda and not a global movement with a global agenda. It is yet to graduate to the level of a mass uprising. It is possible to overcome the threat and break the back of the movement, but a series of well calculated and determined steps have to be taken for this purpose. There are no quick fixes. It is going to be a long-drawn affair.

13

Armed Forces (Special Powers) Act: Should it be Amended or Repealed?

It is reported in the press that, Indian Army Chief has expressed strong reservations regarding any amendment of the Armed Forces (Special Powers) Act, 1958, (AFSPA) contemplated by the Central Government. Earlier, Prime Minister, Manmohan Singh had promised to consider amendments to AFSPA to make it more humane. AFSPA now extends to all the states of North-East except Sikkim. It has also been extended to the state of Jammu and Kashmir since July 1990. The AFSPA was passed to counter growing insurgency in the North-East and it comes into operation after a declaration has been made under Section 2 of the Act that "*the particular area is disturbed*".

Section 4 of the Act gives Armed Forces power to arrest without any warrant a person who has committed a cognizable offence or against whom reasonable suspicion exists that he has committed or about to commit a cognizable offences. It authorizes personnel of the armed forces to use such force as may be necessary to effect the arrest. Other special powers given to the Armed Forces under Section 4 are:

(a) Power to destroy structures used as hideouts, training camps or a place from which attacks are likely to be launched.
(b) Power to open fire even to the extent of causing death if prohibitory order banning assembly of five or more persons or carrying arms or weapons etc. are in force in the disturbed areas.
(c) Power to enter and search premises without warrant to make arrest or recovery of hostages, arms and ammunitions etc.

Section 6 gives members of armed forces discharging duties under the Act, immunity from prosecution and other legal proceedings, except with the previous sanction of the Union Government.

Human rights activist and Civil Society groups have consistently denounced AFSPA as a draconian legislation giving unaccounted and unrestricted power to the security forces to carry out operations in disturbed areas. They are of the view that the Act has been abused and misused by the security forces. According to them, AFSPA has facilitated extra-judicial killing, torture, rape and disappearance which in their turn have fed public anger and disillusionment against the Indian state.

Officers of the armed forces, on the other hand, are of the clear view that diluting of special powers to the security forces under the Act will be counter-productive. In order to function effectively security forces need legal provisions and such laws provide the legal framework, enabling them to conduct proactive operations. Without such laws armed forces in a hostile area cannot function.

Attempts have been made to seek judicial review of the law on the ground that is repugnant to the rights to equality and federal structure of the Constitution. A five-judge Constitution Bench of the Supreme Court held in *Naga Peoples Movement for Human Rights* vs. *Union of India* 1998, held the enactment to be constitutionally valid. The court held though the Act may "*appear to be harsh in the face of it, it was a necessity*". As regard powers vested in the Union Government the Supreme Court noted that Section 3 was amended by Act 7 of 1972 by virtue of which the power to declare an area to be "*a disturbed area*" has also been conferred upon the Central Government. The apex Court also, *inter alia*, concluded that a declaration under Section 3 has to be for a limited period subject to periodic review before the expiry of six months and a person arrested in exercise of power under Section 4(c) of AFSPA should be handed over to the officer in-charge of the nearest police station without delay so that he can be produced before the nearest Magistrate within 24 hours of such arrest excluding the time taken for journey from the place of arrest to the Court of Magistrate.

There was a serious outcry against the Act in 2002 following the custodial death of a woman arrested by the armed forces. Agitation virtually paralyzed Manipur valley and the Union Government then appointed committee under the Chairmanship of Justice Jeevan Reddy, a retired Judge of the Supreme Court to review the AFSPA. The terms of reference of the Commission were to recommend amendments in the Act to bring it in consonance with obligations of the government towards human rights or to replace it with a more humane Act. Thus, implicit behind the setting up of the Committee was the recognition that provisions of the Act needed a fresh look. The Committee after examining the views of various stakeholders came to the conclusion that AFSPA should be repealed. It was of the view that it will be necessary to insert appropriate provisions in the Unlawful Activities (Prevention) Act, 1967 (ULPA) instead of a new legislation.

According to the Committee, the definition of terrorism as provided in the ULPA is quite exhaustive and it also takes into its purview acts committed with intention to threaten the integrity, unity, and security of India. The proposed insertion of Chapter VI(a) in the ULPA will provide the mechanism through which the Armed Forces could be deployed in situations and areas whenever needed. ULPA does not provide for an internal mechanism to ensure accountability of the Armed Forces with a view to guarding against the abuses and excesses by delinquent officers. The Committee recommended creation of a grievance cell in each district of a state where Armed Forces are deployed. This shall be an independent body and shall be competent to enquire into complaints of violation of rights of citizens. The proposed Chapter VI(a) also includes an Appendix that contains the dos and don'ts issued by the army mentioned in the judgment of the Supreme Court.

The Second Administrative Reforms Commission in its report (5th Report – June 2007) has also fully endorsed the recommendation the Jeevan Reddy Committee that AFSPA should be repealed and a new chapter should be inserted in ULPA incorporating provisions regarding the deployment of the Armed Forces in aid of civil power. However, the proposed insertion of Chapter IV(a) should apply only to the North-east.

There is no doubt that the repeal and amendment of AFSPA is a complex and contentious issue. Jeevan Reddy Committee is correct in pointing out that AFSPA, whatever be the reason, has become "*a symbol of oppression and instrument of discrimination and highhandedness*". But the fact cannot be wished away that without deploying the army it is not possible to counter-insurgency in the North-east and Kashmir where the insurgents are aided and abetted by forces across the border. It will not be possible for the local police to take on the well-armed insurgents threatening country's security and integrity.

It is a fact that deployment of the army on a long-term basis in insurgency affected areas of the country like North-east and Kashmir is perhaps unavoidable in the prevailing circumstances. However, prolonged and frequent deployment of Armed Forces for the restoration of public order leads to brutalization of the forces. Armed Forces also become exposed to various temptations and weaknesses. Hence, the legal mechanism under which they function should be clear and specific and aberrant officers responsible for deliberate misuse of force should be held accountable as they sully the fair name of the Armed Forces.

There is an overwhelming desire of the majority of the people of the North-East, as the Jeevan Reddy Committee points out, that "*the army must remain, though the Act should go*". However, without legal safeguards it will not be possible for the armed forces to function effectively. ULP Act does provide a legal framework for deploying Armed Forces or Paramilitary Forces for fighting against terrorist activities in different areas of the country. Section 49 of the Act bars any suit or prosecution against the serving or retired officer of the Armed Forces in respect of any action taken by him in good faith in the course of operations directed towards combating terrorism. ULP Act applies to entire India including North-Eastern states. Hence, the complaint of discrimination will not be valid. This will to some extent go to mitigate the sense of discrimination among the people in the North-East that they are subjected to a draconian law specially enacted for them.

Time has now come for the Union Government to take a clear decision without dithering. Insurgency in the North-east is raging for a long time and numerous allegations of human rights violations of the Armed Forces come before the National Human Rights Commission and other bodies. Section 19 of the Protection of Human Rights Act does not permit NHRC to directly enquire into these complaints, but on the reports received from army authorities it has recommended action against the aberrant officers and compensation to the victims in some cases. Repeal of AFSPA and its replacement by ULPA will not seriously hamper operations of the Armed Forces against the insurgents, but will go to remove a long standing sense of anger and discontent among the people of North-east.

14

Prevention of Torture Bill, 2010

Torture constitutes one of the most grievous violations of human rights. The World Medical Association (WMA) in its Tokyo Declaration (1975) defines torture as a "*deliberate, systematic and wanton infliction of physical or mental suffering by one or more persons acting alone or on the orders of any authority to force another person to yield information, to make a confession or for any other reason*". The definition thus sets out the possible intent of those who practice torture.

The old notion was that the purpose of torture was to make people talk. But one of the objects of torture now is to silence the general population and it is this kind of torture, which is used to curb and threaten democratic systems.

Torture is a crime under International Law and UN Convention Against Torture, 1984 (UNCAT) bans any kind of cruel, inhuman and degrading treatment even in times of war. The convention provides that each state shall take effective, legal, judicial, administrative and other measures to prevent acts of torture and no exceptional circumstances like a state of war or internal political instability or any public emergency be invoked as a justification of torture.

India, after repeated urgings by National Human Rights Commission, signed the Convention in 1997 but did not ratify it. India has thus remained in the company of countries like Sudan, North Korea and Myanmar that have not ratified the Convention. In an expansive interpretation of Article 21 of the Constitution, the right against torture has been judicially recognized as a fundamental right by the Supreme Court and hence delay in ratification has been embarrassing for the country and inexplicable to the people interested in the promotion of human rights.

It is heartening that now at long last, the government has decided to ratify the Convention. Ratification of a Convention requires enabling domestic legislation to implement the provisions of the Convention and provide definition as well as punishment for torture. With this end in view, the government has introduced in the Parliament, the Prevention of Torture Bill, 2010 (PTB) which has been passed by the Lok Sabha and will be taken up for discussion in the Rajya Sabha. The proposed legislation, though undoubtedly a step forward, is in some ways restrictive and inadequate and needs suitable amendments.

The definition of torture in the Bill is narrow and without reference to other forms of cruel, inhuman or degrading treatment or punishment. It also excludes, unlike the definition in the UN Convention Against Torture, (UNCAT) purely mental torture. The Supreme Court in the case of *D.K. Basu* vs. *The State of West Bengal*, has aptly said that the "*torture is calculated assault on human dignity and whenever the human dignity is wounded, the civilization takes a step backward and the flag of humanity on each occasion must fly half mast*".

The definition of torture given in Section 3 of the Bill is that it is an intentional act, which causes grievous hurt, danger to life and limb or health of any person. Section 320 of the Indian Penal Code limits grievous hurt to permanent disability or disfigurement, fracture or dislocation of bones and severe physical pain. Thus, the test of torture propounded in the Bill becomes must stricter and narrower than what is given in UNCAT definition. Hence, some practices like water boarding, beating with rags wrapped in the body or threat of use of violence may not always endanger life, limb, or health. Section 4 of the Bill provides a maximum 10 years of punishment for those convicted of torture, but it does not specify any minimum punishment for a person found guilty of torture. This may result in some cases in a light punishment for perpetrators of torture. To highlight the gravity of the offence and the determination of the government not to countenance torture, the Bill ought to have provided some minimum punishment and thus fetter the discretion of the judges some of whom may take a very tolerant view of torture because of the prevailing situation.

Section 5 of the Bill provides the limitation period of 6 months. If the complaint is not lodged within 6 months of the date on which the alleged offence is committed, the Court shall not take cognizance of the offence. Human Rights activists and many lawyers and academics criticize this limitation period and feel that it provides a layer of protection to the perpetrators of torture. According to them, no limitation period should apply to the serious crimes of torture. But the hard fact remains that delayed complaints are very often tutored or fabricated and an unlimited period of time will encourage free flow of malicious or motivated complaints. The limitation period however, can be extended to one year, as is the practice in respect of complaints before the National Human Rights Commission. Further, to discourage filing of false complaints, there should be provision in the legislation for penalizing those who lodge false complaints with a view to harassing the public servants.

Section 6 of the Bill, prohibits prosecution of a Public servant without previous sanction of the government or authority that employs him. However, as the apex Court has laid down, the power of the government to withhold sanctions can be invoked only when the impugned act has been done in the course of legitimate performance of duties by a public servant. The plea of many NGOs to delete the provision for sanction for public servants who have allegedly committed acts of torture is impractical. It will only expose police officers and public servants to many frivolous and vexatious prosecutions launched with a view to harassing and demoralizing them.

The Bill should have incorporated offences like custodial violence and torture by public servants. Incidence of custodial violence, as highlighted in the reports of the National Human Rights Commission, continues unabated. On an average between 170-180 deaths, take place in police custody and the situation has not improved over the years, despite exhortations of the NHRC and stern rulings of the apex Court. The Bill also should stipulate that an order from a superior officer or public authority cannot be invoked as a justification for torture. Another lacuna in the Bill is that it contains no provisions for compensation of the victims for torture. Article 14 of the UNCAT clearly stipulates that the victim of an act of torture has an enforceable "*right to fair and adequate compensation*". The PTB must provide an enforceable right to reparation for the victims.

Despite these shortcomings, the Bill is a positive step in the right direction. In India, many groups including political leaders and law enforcement officers wrongly and short-sightedly feel that a ban on torture will hamstring the police and security forces in their operations against the terrorists. They justify torture in exceptional circumstances, in cases of "*ticking bomb urgency*". Historical practice however, shows that once a certain degree of force is permitted, interrogators face overwhelming temptations to apply as much force as possible to acquire the sought-for information. There is always the difficulty of determining where to draw the line. It is the danger of "*slippery-slope*" that calls for total ban on torture.

15

Future of Community Policing

The emergence of community policing as an important means of law enforcement has raised pertinent questions about its scope, efficacy and proper implementation. There are also questions about its future. Though community policing has now become a buzzword in law enforcement across the world the term has often been used very imprecisely. There is lack of conceptual clarity even among the senior police officers. Many hold the erroneous view that any form of contact between police and the community comes into the domain of community policing. Some of the key concepts of community policing are thus lost sight of. Community policing involves a paradigm shift in the basic concept of policing. The shift involves recognition by the police that the community is its best resource and greatest ally in the battle against crime and disorder and community partnership helps not only in combating crime but also reducing fear of crime which is also of equally great concern to the community. Giving voice to the community in deciding police programmes and priorities provides useful insights to the police and help them in their work.

Community policing in various forms is now being practiced in different countries of the world. In late 1970s and 80s, police services in England, USA, Japan, Germany, Canada, were experimenting with alternatives to professional bureaucratic models of policing that was widening the gulf between the citizens and police officials. In USA, frustrations with professional bureaucratic models of policing and the specter of rising crimes led to a re-appraisal of existing forms of policing and demand for building and establishing closer linkages between police and the community. It was embraced by many of the police chiefs in 1980s. It gained wide popularity and acceptance when President Clinton made it the centerpiece of his anti-crime campaign. Substantial federal funding for the growth of criminal justice education resulted in the development of empirical research in policing. Many of the research findings challenged the prevailing police practices and beliefs. Federally funded victimization surveys documented the existence of unreported crimes in a big way. Police officers had to acknowledge that only a part of the crimes were being reported to the police by the citizens. To remove this sense of fear and avoidance by the members of the public, the police have to improve their interaction with the community and forge closer links with them. The evolution of community policing in USA also involved association between the police practitioners and the academics. University scholars as well as independent research institutes helped early development of community policing programmes and their refinement. Indeed, many principles of community policing appealed more to the academics than to the police officers. Today, police chiefs in different countries of the world are trying to apply the principles of community policing with varying degrees of success.

Implementation of community policing with considerable success has been achieved both in Japan and Singapore. Both the countries have successfully experimented community policing as basic operating strategies of law enforcement and order maintenance. In Japan, it centres round Koban, a subordinate unit of police station and usually confined to a specified geographical unit. Koban system constitutes the fulcrum of police activities for the maintenance of public peace. Singapore has also successfully followed Japanese model and achieved remarkable success in the implementation of community policing strategies. It has enabled Singapore police to provide better services to the community and there has been remarkable overall improvement in police community relations.

Impact of Community Policing on the Local Residents

Studies by the Brazilian researcher, Tulio Kahn (2002) in Sau Paulo, suggests that following introduction of community policing, members of the community felt safer and have developed greater trust and confidence in the police.[1] Wesley Skogan's studies of community policing in Chicago show that the programmes brought about a positive change in the residents' perception of the police and their activities.[2] However, the researchers also found that the programmes did not have any effect on a Hispanic population who did not notice any improvement in police work. But research studies have also revealed that proactive problem-solving approaches in concert with the community members and the relevant city agencies can bring about reduction in the incidence of specific crimes.

In community policing programmes, there is a mistaken assumption by many police leaders that the public want, partnership with the police. Very often, this is not the case. There is always community's skepticism that they have all heard it before. There is also public fear that cooperation with the police might invite reprisals from the criminals. Without display of genuine commitment and sincerity, the police will not be able to make community policing a success. It has to be borne in mind that public relations and community relations, though often used interchangeably, are not identical. The US President Commission (1966) in the report "*The Challenge of Crime in the Free Society*" makes this distinction. A community relations programme is not a public relations programme to sell the police image to the community. It is not a set of expedients whose purpose is to tranquilize for a time an angry neighbourhood by, for example, suddenly promoting a few Negro officers in the wake of a racial disturbance. It is a long range full-scale effort to acquaint the police and the community with each other's problems and to stimulate action aimed at solving those problems.[3]

In order to be successful, community policing unlike other police initiatives, should not be a top-down arrangement. What makes community policing unique is that it relies on inputs from not just community leaders and blue ribbon panels. It solicits inputs from all stakeholders, encouraging those who are apathetic to become involved. The police not only work out with local public what has to be done, but also ask them to help in appropriate ways. Today around the world, there are hundreds of ways in which local public assist the police in crime prevention work.

Supervision

Proper supervision is essential for the success of community policing. But the old notion that, the police officers have to be constantly guided and directed is to be discarded while implementing community policing programmes. Supervisors must function as mentors and facilitators who can help the patrol officers to properly respond to varieties of service demands.

Equity

The paramount requirement for the success of community policing is respect for all citizens and sensitivity to their needs. Favouritism to one group is definitely going to have very adverse consequences in the working of community policing endeavours. Powerful vocal groups cannot be allowed to exploit community policing to subserve their own needs. There always remains the danger of unequal application of police resources. Local police officers may feel that it is more important to protect "*loud voices than the quiet ones*". One community must not be given preference over another. Equity does not mean equal distribution of police resources and services. Areas where crime rates are high, will always require more police interventions and larger deployment of police resources. But there should be no unfair discrimination.

Training

Training remains key to effective implementation of community policing. In India, some of the community policing programmes have floundered because of inadequately trained clueless police personnel. Same police officers who are performing duties at police stations are being asked to perform the duties of community policing officers. No wonder, they became square pegs in round holes and make a hash of the job assigned to them. Training in community policing should supplement the law enforcement techniques with communication and leadership skills that will encourage participation from the community. There should be training on topics that police men do not learn from academies such as housing problems, roles and responsibilities of other departmental agencies etc.

For continued advancement of community policing, there is need for solid evidence base. There should be strong evidence base to support the wisdom of community policing rather than the hyperbole that currently surrounds it. Besides, guiding what is implemented; the research will guide the police organizations to justify the identified priorities and commitments when meeting the demand for public accountability. Police organizations in order to function successfully must develop the institutional capacity to understand the impact of their own strategies and use their knowledge to provide higher measure of safety, and reassurance to the public.[4]

Challenges

Organizational control and implementation of community policing encounter some of the following challenges :

1. There can be erosion of support for community policing if the community expectations are not fulfilled. Criticisms are levelled that community policing may detract the core functions of the police and make it soft in crime control. Many including some senior police officers denigrate Community Policing Officers (CPOs) as "*lollipop cops*". The fact, however, is overlooked that real community policing does not neglect or ignore the law enforcement role of the police. These socialization duties are performed in addition to the law enforcement functions and not as substitutes for them. Indeed, successful community policing will go to improve and enhance the quality of police operations by increasing cooperation with the community.
2. Critics have voiced the fear that community policing may undermine police professionalism. This criticism will be valid if the community policing tends to turn the police officers into social workers. Community policing is first and foremost a crime prevention effort. Investigative policing has to continue side by side with community policing. Indeed, community

policing should improve and refine police operations by forging closer links with the community.

3. There is also the danger of the political empowerment of the community-based officers. An officer may become so involved in the community that he/she becomes a political advocate instead of a community resource. This impairs his capacity for genuine community policing work.
4. There are dangers of internal strains and tensions within the police when the emphasis shifts from traditional activities to the new police initiatives. But community policing is not, and should not be, an independent entity within the organization. Community policing is not meant to substitute for other forms of policing but a complement to other efforts. Community policing works best when it is found not to operate in isolation.
5. Lack of honest evaluation hampers advancement of community policing practices. As a result, lessons are not drawn from the omissions of the past. In India, many of the community policing projects have not achieved necessary degree of success because they have seldom been properly and objectively evaluated. In consequence, changes and modifications of the programmes in the light of the evaluations have not taken place.
6. It has also been noticed that community policing is more successful in well organized and the cohesive communities which need community policing least. Mobilization of support in disorganized communities

separated by caste, creed and religious divisions is far more difficult.

Police leaders should not allow the political leaders and the public to develop unrealistic expectations for community policing in respect of crime prevention and order maintenance. Community policing is not a quick fix. It calls for long-term commitment. Success can be achieved only through a series of gradual improvements. Taking into account the positive, negative and uncertain forces affecting the institutionalization of community policing in India, it seems that in the coming decades there will be further expansion of community-based policing activities. The progress will be somewhat slow and incremental because neither the political nor the police leaders are in favour of empowering the citizens and making the police accountable to the community.

References

1. Tulio Kahn,(2002) "Civilian Oversight of police", in http://www.altus.org/altus/research_tools/bibliography_hot_topics.
2. Wesley Skogan, "Community Policing : The Chicago Styles", New York and Oxford, Oxford University Press, 1997.
3. US President's Commission on Law Enforcement and Administration of Justice. The Challenge of a Crime in a Free Society, p.100.
4. Bayley, D. (1999) "Capacity Building in Law Enforcement Trends and Issues in Crime and Criminal Justice", July, 1999, No. 123, Canberra: Australian Institute of Criminology.

16

Missing Children

Reports in the press that 60,000 children below 18 years were found missing in 2009 as compared to 44,000 in 2004 should be a matter of serious public concern. Earlier, a research study sponsored by National Human Rights Commission and conducted by the Institute of Social Sciences, 2005, revealed that any given year an average of 44,000 children are reported missing and of them 11,000 remain untraced. This, however, is just a tentative and unrealistic estimate because data collected from police records are inadequate and incorrect. Many cases are not reported, or if reported, not registered by the police. Missing children end up in a variety of pathetic situations – killed and buried in neighbours' backyards (as in Nithari serial killings), work as forced labour in illegal factories/ homes, exploited as sex slaves or forced as child beggars in begging rackets.

NHRC's "*Action Research on Trafficking*" has shown through several case studies the linkage between "*trafficking and persons reported missing.*" Many of these missing children are trafficked for commercial sexual exploitation, or forced labour and other forms of abuse. Unfortunately, the police seldom properly investigate cases of missing children. Normally, investigation of a crime commences with the registration of an F.I.R. (First Information Report) in the police station. Registration of an FIR, presupposes a cognizable offence. But in the case of a missing person or child, no formal FIR is registered in the police station; only a missing person's entry is made in the police station diary. The Station House Officer forwards the information to the Superintendent or Deputy Superintendent of police who in turn forwards it to the Chief of the police. Local police officials publicize the particulars of the missing person in the media by circulating available identification details and photographs. After this, no further serious efforts are made to locate the missing children. There are no sustained follow-up efforts to locate the missing children.

At police headquarters, information regarding missing persons are lodged with Missing Person Bureau, a wing of the State CID. They in turn forward the message to the State Crime Bureau and to the Missing Person Wing of the National Crime Records Bureau (NCRB) in New Delhi, which operates under the control of the Ministry of Home Affairs. NCRB acts as a documentation centre. It does neither investigate nor does it monitor or facilitate recovery of missing children. Police stations also do not give feed-backs to the NCRB whether the missing child is traced or returned. Thus, despite being the missing national repository of Crime Data, NCRB remains unaware of children who are traced and those who remain untraced. Further, there is no analysis of problem of missing children in the *Annual Crime in India* report published by NCRB.

Thus, virtually under the existing arrangements no serious efforts are being made to trace the missing children. This constitutes a big loophole in our existing arrangements of prevention and control of crimes against children. I still recall with some measure of satisfaction that when I was posted as Range DIG, in Rourkela, Orissa, I could help an anxious father who was an engineer in Rourkela Steel Plant to trace out his only son because I could detail an officer exclusively for investigation of this case. The child could be traced by the investigating officer in a Mumbai dhaba after a week. However, this is not possible in every case because of man-power constraints.

The Supreme Court in the writ petition No. 610/1996, Horilal, Commissioner of Police, Delhi, issued a number of useful guidelines with regard to steps to be taken for tracing out missing and kidnapped minor girls and children. These guidelines include publishing the photographs of missing persons/children in the newspapers, enquiries about missing children in educational institutions, issuing hue and cry notices and setting up a multi-task force under state CID for locating missing girls and women.

In USA, private non-profit organizations like National Centre for Missing and Exploited Children (NCMEC) provide free services to the families of kidnapped and sexually exploited children. It also serves as a clearing house for information about missing and exploited children. In India, there are NGOs like Children India Foundation, (CIF), National Centre for Missing Children (NCMC) who have hosted Websites displaying photos of missing children for whom the police are conducting enquiries.

Unfortunately, there is no systematic coordination and cooperation between the police and NGOs dedicated to this endeavour. Indeed, efforts to trace out missing children remain *ad hoc* and slipshod.

There is an urgent need for a National Data Base and monitoring Centre. For this, NCRB should establish a National Tracking System that could encompass locating and tracking missing children at grassroots levels. The database has to be updated on a regular and systematic basis and the information, which is gathered, has to be properly disseminated. It may be mentioned in this connection that Delhi police has introduced since 2006 computerization of missing persons data. Before computerization of data, tracing of missing persons was about 25 per cent. It jumped to 73 per cent in 2006 and about 80 per cent of missing children were traced. This is a notable achievement. Global display of available information has helped not only the police but the general public also.

As per the orders of the Delhi High Court, a cell relating to missing persons/children has been set-up in the Central Bureau of Investigation and entrusted with the task of coordinating efforts all over the country for tracing missing persons and children. However, due to resource constraint, the cell is not functioning effectively. It is necessary to strengthen the cell in order to enhance its capacity to coordinate and investigate criminal cases relating to missing children.

The Committee set-up by the NHRC under one of its members P. C. Sharma has given a bold suggestion that preliminary enquiries into cases of missing persons could be outsourced by the police to NGOs who are willing to undertake this task. Such NGOs can be notified by the State Government. MHA may issue appropriate guidelines to the NGOs in this regard. Synergy between law enforcement agency and the NGOs will be of great use and help in this regard. In the words of the NHRC committee, missing children constitute "*a veritable black hole in law enforcement*". Unfortunately, the police have so far failed to acknowledge gravity of the problem and steps to trace out or recover missing children remain a matter of low priority. In order to successfully grapple with the growing menace, there is need for strong political commitment, mobilization of resources and coordination between police, social service, administration and other institutions of civil society.

17

Police Reforms: A Bumpy Road

The Supreme Court's judgment in the case of *Prakash Singh* vs. *Union of India* (2006) is a historic one and marks a defining moment in the history of Indian Police. The apex Court endorsed the view of National Police Commission (1978-81), that Indian Police has become the hand maiden of the political party in power and totally alienated from the people. It has also become professionally incompetent. The NPC after a careful study of the police workload could find that the police officers spend only thirty per cent of their time in investigation of cases. And most of their time is devoted in VIP duties, court attendance and other miscellaneous chores. No wonder that their core functions, namely prevention and detection of crime, only get step-motherly attention. Perfunctory investigation by the police has drawn adverse comments from the courts in many cases. Police Investigation in the case of Dr. Vinayak Sen, *prima facie* appears to be slipshod and the life sentence imposed on him by the court is shocking and perverse.

For the improvement in the functioning of the criminal justice system, there is categorical need for systemic reforms in the police. The National Police Commission (better know as *Dharamvira Commission*) made sound practical recommendations for police reforms, which are relevant even today. Unfortunately, the Union Government deliberately took no steps to implement these recommendations. In fact, the report of the National Police Commission was put on a backburner. The Supreme Court stepped into the breach in 1996, when two former DGPs filed a PIL before the apex Court, asking it to direct the State Governments to implement the recommendations of the National Police Commission. It was argued that non-implementation of the recommendations of the NPC was adversely affecting the criminal justice administration in the country. The Supreme Court in 2006 issued clear directives to the Centre and the States to implement the recommendations of the National Police Commission with a view to insulating the police from extraneous pressures and influence. The court took the view that time has come for issuance of appropriate directions for police reforms for immediate compliance till a Model Police Act is enacted by the Central Government.

The seven point directives of the Supreme Court include:

(a) A fixed tenure for at least two years for Director General of Police (DGP) unless promoted or removed on disciplinary grounds. The Chief Minister will no longer be able to remove or transfer any inconvenient DGP and pick up a pliant officer of his choice.

(b) Separation of the law and order wing and investigation wing of the police.

(c) Setting up of a Police Establishment Board to decide on transfer, posting and service related matters of the officers up to the rank Deputy Superintendent of Police

(d) Setting up of State Security Commission in every state to insure that the state government does not exercise unwarranted influence and pressures on the police.

(e) Establishing a National Security Commission for selection and placements of chiefs of Central Police Organizations.

The cornerstone of police reforms directed by the apex Court is the setting up of State Security Commission in every state to ensure that the state government does not exercise unwarranted influence or pressure on the police. The State Security Commission will be headed by Home Minister or the Chief Minister, but the independence of the Commission has sought to be ensured by the inclusion of the leader of opposition, a retired sitting judge and some important non-political citizens. The court has further ordered that a Police Complaints Authority (PCA) will be set-up in every district headed by a retired judge to enquire into allegations of serious misconduct by the police. The judgment of the Supreme Court is historic. It will have significant impact on the administration of Indian police in the coming years and may usher in a new dawn for the Indian police.

Unfortunately, many state governments are dragging their feet and trying to stonewall police reforms under various pretexts. They are not at all prepared to slacken their iron grip over the police with a view to misuse it for partisan ends. Majority of the states have averred that though they support the spirit of reforms, they object to many of the directives of the court. States like Gujarat, Nagaland, Karnataka, Andhra Pradesh have questioned the *raison d'etre* of the State Security Commission. Some have also brazenly stated that they exert no unwarranted influence over the police. Many states have enacted new Police Acts. But the new Acts that have been passed dilute the core systemic reforms prescribed by the Supreme Court. Some of the states have set-up State Security Commissions but packed them with yes-men and excluded the leader of the opposition to deprive these bodies of a bi-partisan character. To retain political control over the police, they have indeed made some cosmetic changes and not meaningful systemic police reforms.

The Supreme Court, has however, cracked its whip over police reforms. It set up a three member monitoring committee with Justice K.T. Thomas, a former Supreme Court Judge, as its chairperson. The Committee examined the affidavits filed by different states regarding measures taken by them to implement the apex Court's directives. It also examined the New Police Acts passed by some states after the Supreme Court's judgment of 2006 to find out if they are in keeping with the letter and spirit of the directives of the apex Court. The monitoring committee in its report has castigated the non-compliance of the directives of the apex Court by the states. The Police Complaint Authorities have not been created in most of the states that have enacted new laws. The Committee checked up the ground realities regarding the implementation of the directives in respect of four states, namely, Uttar Pradesh, Karnataka, West Bengal and Maharashtra and found that level of compliance of the Supreme Court's directives in these states is poor, if not dismal. It deplored the indifference displayed by the states and asked the Supreme Court to view seriously non-compliance of police reforms by the states.

The Supreme Court has taken the matter seriously. A bench headed by the Chief Justice adopted a no-nonsense approach and chided West Bengal government for putting the Health Minister as the head of the State Security Commission. The Bench also severely pulled up the government of UP for not segregating law and order and investigation wings of the police. Indeed, the Supreme Court has taken up the implementation of its directives in a serious manner has said that its "*order will not remain in limbo*". Time frames were given to states to report compliance of various points. Nevertheless, the path of police reforms is going to be bumpy. Political masters will try to scuttle meaningful reforms that will make police neutral and apolitical. Sustained campaign by senior police leaders, members of civil society and media is necessary to overcome their resistance and usher in much-needed police reforms.

18

Collegium System of Appointment of Judges

Against the backdrop of the raging controversy over the elevation of the Karnataka High Court Chief Justice, P. B. Dinakaran to the Supreme Court, the Bar Association of the Delhi High Court and the Supreme Court in a joint letter to the Union Law Minister has sought the discontinuation of the apex Court collegium for appointment of the judges of Supreme Court and High Courts. The letter says that the Collegium system of appointment of judges has not only proved to be a failure but encouraged lack of transparency and favouritism. Indeed, judicial probity is closely linked with the proper appointment of judges in the higher courts. The health of judiciary depends much on the people appointed as judges. The previous system of judicial appointments by the executive (1953-93) was substituted by judicial collegium of five senior judges by the apex Court's decision in the Second Judges case.

Article 124 of the Constitution of India vests the power of appointment of the Chief Justices and Judges of the Supreme Court in the President. The Constitution provides that the President will make these appointments in consultation with the Judges of the High Court and Supreme Court that he deems necessary. The Constitutional provision speaks of "*after consultation*" and not "*in consultation*" in the case of appointment of judges other than the Chief Justice of India. The appointment of High Court Judges is also made by the President in consultation with the Chief Justice of India and the Governor of the State.

In *S.P. Gupta's* case known as First Judges case, the Court by a majority ruled that Article 217(1) puts all the Constitutional functionaries in the same pedestal and no primacy was given to the Chief Justice of India. *S.P. Gupta's* case did not deal with the appointment of Judges in the Supreme Court. In 1993 in Second Judges case, the Supreme Court ruled that the recommendation of the Chief Justice of India along with four seniormost colleagues is determinative and binding on the President. This was almost an attempt by the judiciary to re-write the law through this judgment. The new construction makes the Supreme Court and High Court virtually undemocratic. According to a former Law Minister under the present Collegium system, merit has been ignored while give and take has thrived. Even some of the former Chief Justices who believed in giving power exclusively to the judiciary in the matter of appointment and transfer of Judges have revised their opinion.

In July 1999, the President sought court's opinion on certain issues relating to the appointment of Supreme Court Judges and transfer of High Court Judges. Nine Judges

Bench of the Supreme Court (Presidential References, AIR, 1999, SC) reiterated that primacy is to be given to the opinion of the Chief Justice as laid down in 1993 judgment, but also stipulated that the Collegium should make the decision in consensus, and unless the opinion of the collegium is in conformity with that of the Chief Justice of India, no recommendation is to be made. The Chief Justice of India should consult a collegium of four seniormost judges of the apex Court and even if the two Judges give an adverse opinion, the Chief Justice of India should not send the recommendation to the government.

It has been found that the present system in the selection of Judges is not transparent and often characterized by gross favouritism. Without a transparent procedure of selection, the selected Judges will not command public confidence. Justice Krishna Ayer has called the present arrangement "incestuous" because the Judges only react and talk to one another of their own kind. Right from 1950, appointments of Judges have been broadly based upon the recommendations of the Chief Justice of Supreme Court and High Court except during the emergency. It was rare that any appointments were made without the concurrence of the Chief Justice.

There is now a consensus that a National Judicial Council should be constituted for the selection of Judges. The selection mechanism should be more broad based. The argument that to involve persons other than the Judges in selection of the Judges, will bring into play extraneous pressure is somewhat simplistic.

Matters connected with appointment and misdemeanour of higher judiciary should be dealt with by an independent body using transparent procedure instead of the present and unsatisfactory arrangement shrouded in mystery. The appointments of Judges have to be above suspicion and the best way is to introduce transparency. The names of those proposed to be appointed as Judges may be put up on the Court's website and time given to the public in case anyone has an objection to any name. The Parliamentary Standing Committee of Law and Justice recommended doing away with the existing mechanism of collegium. It said that the collegium system has been a disaster and needed to be done away with. Former Chief Justice of India, A.M. Ahmadi who had opposed the creation of the collegium system by writing a dissenting judgment has favoured reversion to pre-collegium mechanism as there are serious concerns about the effectiveness of the present system.

There is no doubt that the present system has encouraged nepotism and many ill-qualified judges with poor records have been elevated. For example, Justice Ashok Kumar was elevated as an additional Judge in Tamil Nadu in April 2003. The Collegium of the Supreme Court Judges unanimously decided not to confirm him as a permanent Judge because of adverse reports against him. He was however, confirmed in April 2007 on the recommendation of the Chief Justice of India. The worst example of the collegium system was the appointment of Soumitra Sen as Judge at Kolkata High Court in 2006 even as he faced allegations of having misappropriated

Rs. 50 lakh (5 Million) while serving as a Court appointed lawyer in 1993 in a dispute between two Public Sector companies. The Collegium cleared him for appointment without bothering to check his credentials even when the entire record was available in the Court itself. There is often lack of information with the collegium on the candidates, which it considers for appointment. In every HC, the Chief Justice is from outside the state as per the policy of the government. The senior-most Judges who form the collegium are also from outside the state. As a result, more often than not, the appointments suffer from lack of adequate information. The Judicial appointments is not a part-time job that members of the collegium can perform after doing their judicial work of deciding cases.

The Law Commission had, *suo motu*, studied the law on the subject, as well as various recommendations of the Parliamentary Standing Committees and the law of foreign jurisdiction like the US, Australia, Canada and Kenya where the executive is the sole authority to appoint the Judges or the executive appoints them in consultation with the Chief Justice of the Country. The Chairman of the Law Commission, Justice A.R Lakshmanan has correctly observed that the Judges constituting the collegium – a panel headed by CJI – are not conversant with the names and antecedents of the candidates for judicial posts and more often than not, appointments suffer due to lack of adequate information.

In South Africa, the new Constitution has adopted a Judicial Commission for selection of Judges. The Law Minister is formally consulted and he gives his comments on the appointees and recommendees of the judiciary. The comments of the Law Minister are considered with respect and attention. Earlier, during the NDA rule the then Law Minister, Arun Jaitley in 2003 in the aftermath of the sex scam that led to the resignation of Delhi High Court Judge Saumit Mukherjee came up with the Constitutional Amendment Bill proposing a National Judicial Commission that tried to involve non-judicial members not only in appointment of Judges but also in disciplining them. Instead of improving on the Bill the former Law Minister, H.R. Bhardwaj rolled back the reform of involving other stakeholders. By proposing National Judicial Council consisting only serving Judges, he acceded to the judiciary's claim that any effort to open up the process of judicial accountability would compromise judicial independence. The Bill is pending before the standing committee of the Parliament since August 2007. The present Law Minister has now proposed to bring a comprehensive Bill on Judicial Standards and Accountability to deal with various issues and maladies afflicting the judiciary.

19

Imperative Need for an Effective Lokpal

Anna Hazare's crusade has brought in sharp focus the issue of corruption in public life. Unfortunately, the functioning of the Joint Committee comprising 5 Ministers and 5 Members of the civil society to draft the Lokpal Bill may be derailed by the controversies that have now erupted. There is indeed a well orchestrated smear campaign against some of the members of the civil society group which seems to enjoy covert political support. Some leading social activists are also very critical of Anna Hazare and dub his movement as authoritarian and unconstitutional. The overriding objective of preparing a powerful Lokpal Bill to be passed by the Parliament is being lost sight of.

Anna's campaign against corruption elicited tremendous public response all over the country because of the lack of political will to combat it vigorously. The Lokpal Bill was first passed in Lok Sabha in 1969 but could not get through the Rajya Sabha. The Bill was subsequently introduced 7 times more in the Parliament but could not be passed. This happened mainly due to lack of political will. Lokpal Bill 2010 drafted by the Law Ministry sought to create a toothless

Lokpal by providing that the Lokpal shall not enquire into any allegations of corruption against any member of either House of Parliament, unless permitted by the Speaker or Chairman, Rajya Sabha. The Speaker of the Lok Sabha or the Chairmen of Rajya Sabha will determine what action has to be taken and this implies his authority to reject the report of Lokpal. Further, Lokpal will have no police powers and cannot register FIRs or proceed with criminal investigation. The official Lok Pal Bill excludes the bureaucrats, despite the known nexus between the civil servants and the political leaders. Certain Prime Ministerial actions will also be beyond scrutiny as to where they related to external affairs, security and defense. Thus, corruption in defense deals is sought to be kept out of Lokpal's purview.

Indeed, it is common experience that exposure by recommendations which leaves out follow-up action by the government lacks teeth and shields corruption. This has been proved by India's Lok Ayukta experience as well as that of the NHRC. The new Lokpal Bill has to be drafted carefully so that it creates a workable and viable as well as an effective mechanism to fight against corruption. The suggestion in the Jan Lokpal Bill drafted by civil society to include in the selection committee besides Judges of the Supreme Court and the Chief Justices of High Court, all Nobel laureates of Indian origin and last three Magassey awardees is impractical and unacceptable. In the selection committee there should be representatives of the government, leaders of opposition, Judges, as well as some eminent people of unquestionable integrity from civil society to be selected by the Chief Justice of India.

Jan Lokpal Bill seeks to provide wide charter of functions to Lokpal. Besides receiving complaints of omission and commission which are punishable under the Prevention of Corruption Act, the Lokpal will receive complaints of misconduct by public servants, complaints from whistle-blowers and various other grievances from the public. It will have the power to initiate prosecution against public servants, impose penalties under CCA Conduct Rules, blacklist any firm, company or contractor involved in acts of corruption, take necessary action and provide protection to whistle-blowers etc. One can well visualize that with this wide array of functions Lokpal will be inundated with complaints from all-over the country and it will be a herculean job for him to deal with them satisfactorily. Its fate will be similar to that of the National Human Rights Commission which now receives annually more than 70,000 complaints from all-over the country and not able to deal with them properly, causing disappointment and frustration among the complainants. It would be perhaps prudent if the remit of Lokpal is restricted to acts of corruption by politicians and the bureaucrats in view of the nexus between the two.

The noteworthy features of corruption in India are first, it occurs upstream and not downstream and this corruption at the top distorts fundamental decisions about policies, projects and developments. Second, corruption in India has wings and not wheels. Very often corruption gains are smuggled to safer havens abroad and not ploughed back to domestic production and investments. Third, corruption often leads to promotion and not to prison. In advanced

Western countries as well as in some countries of south Asia notably, Japan and South Korea, even top leaders are not spared. The Italian Prime Minister, Bettino Craxy had to live in exile in Tunisia due to corruption charges at home. Unfortunately, in India corrupt persons are too powerful and beyond accountability. One of the reasons why corruption has become all-pervasive is because it has become a high reward and low risk activity. Very few public servants including political leaders get punished. Some kind of "*law of jungle*", as a sociologist puts it, prevails. In my long career in law enforcement I have seldom seen any political leader or IAS or IPS officer charged, tried, convicted and then served a jail sentence under Prevention of Corruption Act. If the Lokpal after thorough investigation succeeds in prosecuting and convicting some influential leaders or top bureaucrats and sends them to jail, the effect will be electric. It will send a resounding message that corruption will not be tolerated. There is every likelihood that efforts will be made to stifle the functioning of Lokpal through writ petitions. Already a PIL petition has been filed questioning the validity of the joint committee. The High Courts' and the Supreme Courts' power of judicial review cannot be taken away but perhaps some provisions in the Bill are necessary so that decisions of the Lokpal can only be challenged in the Supreme Court.

Further, corruption cases launched by Lokpal have to be tried in special fast track courts. Lokpal should not perhaps probe into complaints of corruption against the judges. This should be left to be dealt with by the National Judicial Commission comprising Judges as well as outsiders. Enquiries by Lokpal into complaints against Judges may open up wider issues of independence of the judiciary etc. Now Anna Hazare has also agreed that cases of corruption in higher judiciary should be beyond the pale of Lok Pal's purview.

There is no doubt that a strong and effective Lokpal Bill will provide a successful instrument for combating corruption. However, along with the creation of a powerful institution of Lokpal there should be other essential reforms like electoral reforms and police reforms. The National Commission to review the working of the Constitution recommended that Representation of Peoples' Act should be amended to provide that any person charged with any offence punishable with imprisonment which may extend up to 5 years or more should be disqualified from contesting election, and if a political party puts up such a candidate with knowledge of his antecedents, it should be de-recognized and de-registered.

Special Courts should be set-up for speedy trial and disposal of such cases. At present 4,000 cases are pending in different courts of the country under the Prevention of Corruption Act. Since 1990, Central Vigilance Commission granted sanction against 100 civil servants and only 1 has been so far convicted in the court of law. Supreme Court's directives for police reforms, i.e. insulating the police from extraneous influence, have not been implemented by different state governments under various pretexts. Further, Lokpal has to be incorruptible as well as accountable. Its functioning has to be completely transparent and any complaint against any officer of Lokpal has to be investigated, and the officer if found corrupt should be dismissed forthwith. There should be checks and balances over the functioning of Lokpal. All over the world, the Ombudsman or Lokpal reports to legislature, though it functions independently. Similar provisions must also exist in the Lokpal Bill.

A powerful Lokpal Bill is absolutely necessary because India is now ranked as one of the most corrupt countries of the world. A survey published in March 23, 2011 by PERC, a Shanghai-based consultancy, shows that of 16 Asian countries assessed, India now ranks 4th most corrupt in the eyes of 1725 businessmen questioned. Corruption in India is being considered worse than that of China or Vietnam and it is embarrassingly grouped with the likes of Cambodia. It is also a fact as, INFOSYS's Narayan Murthy says, reduced corruption means a rise in GDP growth, translating into higher returns in terms of revenue generation and job creation. Graft is scaring away foreign business, and investors are more negative than they were 4 years ago.

Though criticisms against Anna Hazare's movement that it is anti-democratic and disparate etc. are now being voiced from different quarters, the fact remains that he has been able to unleash righteous public indignation against corruption. A shift in public tolerance for corruption is taking place and the demand for setting up institutions for ensuring accountability and transparency of government activities has gathered momentum. Unfortunately, there are looming fears that there would be a strong rearguard action by powerful interests to stall or dilute any effective bill creating a powerful no nonsense Lokpal. If this happens it will be a sad betrayal of people's hope and expectations.

Index